Latin

FOR COMMON ENTRANCE

13+
LEVEL 1

Exam Practice Questions

R.C. Bass

GALORE PARK

AN HACHETTE UK COMPANY

About the author

Bob Bass taught at prep schools in Somerset, Kenya and Sussex before moving in 1987 to Orwell Park, Ipswich, where he is Head of Classics and Senior Master. He has served on the editorial board of the *Journal of Classics Teaching* and on the Council of the Joint Association of Classical Teachers. For 12 years he edited the SATIPS Classics Broadsheet, and has been IAPS' Subject Leader and then Subject Adviser in Classics. He is the Chief Setter of ISEB's Common Entrance and Common Academic Scholarship Latin papers, proof-reader for their Greek papers, and an IGCSE examiner. He is the author of various Latin and Greek resources targeted at young learners.

Every effort has been made to trace all copyright holders, but if any have been inadvertently overlooked, the Publishers will be pleased to make the necessary arrangements at the first opportunity.

Although every effort has been made to ensure that website addresses are correct at time of going to press, Galore Park cannot be held responsible for the content of any website mentioned in this book. It is sometimes possible to find a relocated web page by typing in the address of the home page for a website in the URL window of your browser.

Hachette UK's policy is to use papers that are natural, renewable and recyclable products and made from wood grown in sustainable forests. The logging and manufacturing processes are expected to conform to the environmental regulations of the country of origin.

Orders: please contact Bookpoint Ltd, 130 Milton Park, Abingdon, Oxon OX14 4SB. Telephone: (44) 01235 827720. Fax: (44) 01235 400454. Email education@bookpoint.co.uk Lines are open from 9 a.m. to 5 p.m., Monday to Saturday, with a 24-hour message answering service. Visit our website at www.galorepark.co.uk for details of other revision guides for Common Entrance, examination papers and Galore Park publications.

ISBN: 978 1 4718 5345 6

© Robert C. Bass 2015

First published in 2015 by
Galore Park Publishing Ltd,
An Hachette UK Company
Carmelite House
50 Victoria Embankment
London EC4Y 0DZ
www.galorepark.co.uk

Impression number   10 9 8 7 6 5 4 3 2

Year   2019 2018

Typeset in India

Printed in the United Kingdom

A catalogue record for this title is available from the British Library.

Latin
FOR COMMON ENTRANCE

**13+
LEVEL 1**

Exam
Practice
Questions

Contents

Introduction

This collection of practice exercises, previously published as *Latin Practice Exercises Level 1*, is designed to provide material for pupils in the early stages of learning Latin, particularly those preparing for the ISEB Common Entrance examination at Level 1.

It provides extensive material for translation, both into and out of Latin, giving pupils the opportunity to revise or consolidate skills they have learnt in those courses.

The vocabulary, grammar and syntax are deliberately geared to the Level 1 syllabus for Common Entrance. In writing the exercises, however, it was found useful to include the following words which are not required for Level 1:

from Level 2: **celeriter, Graecus, heri, hodie, nihil, punio, quoque**

from Level 3: **lente**

non-Common Entrance words: **cena, discipulus, fleo, sedeo, villa**

An answer book, including mark schemes for the exercises, is available separately. Pupils progressing beyond Level 1 may find the companion volumes for Levels 2 and 3, available from Galore Park, useful. For a full list of resources available visit www.galorepark.co.uk

Nicholas Oulton
Series Editor

→ The syllabus and your exams

For Common Entrance Latin, you will sit an exam lasting one hour. You will choose one of the three levels, Level 1, Level 2 or Level 3, as agreed with your teacher.

The format of each level is the same, but the material gets harder. In each level, there are four questions worth a total of 75 marks, as follows:

Question 1 (15 marks)

A short passage of Latin will be set, on which you will be asked to answer eight to ten questions, testing your understanding of the passage. You will not be expected to write a translation of the passage, but clearly you need to have translated it in your head, in order to answer the questions.

Question 2 (30 marks)

Another, slightly longer passage will be set, continuing the story from the passage in Question 1. You will be asked to translate this passage, writing your translation on alternate lines.

Question 3 (20 marks)

Another short passage of Latin will be set, continuing the story from the earlier two passages. Questions will be set, testing your knowledge of Latin grammar and how the language works. You will not be asked to translate this passage, but again you will find it difficult to answer the questions unless you have translated it for yourself.

The questions will fall into the following types:

- From the passage give, in Latin, one example of: (an adjective, a preposition followed by the accusative, a noun in the genitive, a verb in the imperfect tense, etc.)
- **erat** (line 2). In which tense is this verb? What is the 1st person singular of the present tense of this verb?
- **pueros** (line 4). In which case is this noun? Why is this case used?

- **vocaverunt** (line 5). What does this word mean? What is the connection between **vocaverunt** and the English word *vocation*?
- **necat** (line 5) means *he kills*. How would you say in Latin *he was killing* (imperfect tense)?

And last but not least:
- Using the vocabulary given, translate the following two short sentences into Latin.

   Most candidates lose the majority of their marks on Question 3 by falling into the trap of thinking they do not need to translate the passage. They simply guess the answers. To answer a question such as 'in which case is the word **templum** in line 3?', you have to have translated the sentence in which the word **templum** is. Otherwise you will simply be guessing, particularly with a word such as **templum**, which could be any of nominative, vocative or accusative singular.

Question 4 (10 marks)

You will be set eight questions on four areas: Roman domestic life; the city of Rome; the army and Roman Britain; and Greek mythology. Each question will have two parts, part (i) and part (ii). You select **one** question, and answer both parts of it. Examples are given below:

The city of Rome

   (c) (i) Tell the story of Cloelia.

      (ii) Which elements of this story would the Romans have found particularly admirable? Explain your answer.

Greek mythology

   (h) (i) Tell the story of Odysseus' encounter with the Cyclops.

      (ii) Describe two qualities which Odysseus displayed in this encounter.

   These are two of the eight questions that might have been set, labelled (a) to (h). If you had chosen to do the one labelled (c) above, you would have done both part (i) and part (ii) of that question.

→ Tips on revising

Get the best out of your brain

- Give your brain plenty of oxygen by exercising. You can only revise effectively if you feel fit and well.
- Eat healthy food while you are revising. Your brain works better when you give it good fuel.
- Think positively. Give your brain positive messages so that it will want to study.
- Keep calm. If your brain is stressed, it will not operate effectively.
- Take regular breaks during your study time.
- Get enough sleep. Your brain will carry on sorting out what you have revised while you sleep.

Get the most from your revision

- Don't work for hours without a break. Revise for 20–30 minutes, then take a five-minute break.
- Do good things in your breaks: listen to your favourite music, eat healthy food, drink some water, do some exercise or juggle. Don't read a book, watch TV or play on the computer; it will conflict with what your brain is trying to learn.
- When you go back to your revision, review what you have just learnt.
- Regularly review the material you have learnt.

Get motivated

- Set yourself some goals and promise yourself a treat when the exams are over.
- Make the most of all the expertise and talent available to you at school and at home. If you don't understand something, ask your teacher to explain.
- Get organised. Find a quiet place to revise and make sure you have all the equipment you need.
- Use year and weekly planners to help you organise your time so that you revise all subjects equally.
- Use topic and subject checklists to help you keep on top of what you are revising.

Know what to expect in the exam

- Use past papers to familiarise yourself with the format of the exam.
- Make sure you understand the language examiners use.

Before the exam

- Have all your equipment and pens ready the night before.
- Make sure you are at your best by getting a good night's sleep before the exam.
- Have a good breakfast in the morning.
- Take some water into the exam if you are allowed.
- Think positively and keep calm.

During the exam

- Have a watch on your desk. Work out how much time you need to allocate to each question and try to stick to it.
- Make sure you read and understand the instructions on the front of the exam paper.
- Allow some time at the start to read and consider the questions carefully before writing anything.
- Read every question at least twice. Don't rush into answering before you have a chance to think about it.

→ What is Latin?

Latin was the language spoken by the ancient Romans. The city of Rome was situated in the area of Italy called *Latium* which is where Latin gets its name from. The name still survives in the Italian football team *Lazio* (pronounced *Lat-zee-oh*).

Rome started off as a small settlement on the banks of the River Tiber. It gradually became more powerful by conquering nearby villages, then all of Italy, then countries beyond Italy. The area ruled by Rome, which is about the same size as modern Europe and northern Africa, was called the *Roman Empire*.

The Latin spoken by people in different parts of the Roman Empire developed over hundreds of years and gradually turned into modern languages such as Italian, French, Spanish and Portuguese. You will find that a knowledge of Latin is very useful if you ever come to learn one of these modern languages.

Many English words come from Latin as well, and you will find that your English spelling and grammar will improve as you do more Latin.

Here is a table of the numbers from 1 to 10 in Latin and three modern European languages. The languages here are called *Romance* languages, because they are closely connected with Latin, the language of the Romans.

	Latin	Italian	Spanish	French
1	unus	uno	uno	un
2	duo	due	dos	deux
3	tres	tre	tres	trois
4	quattuor	quattro	cuatro	quatre
5	quinque	cinque	cinco	cinq
6	sex	sei	seis	six
7	septem	sette	siete	sept
8	octo	otto	ocho	huit
9	novem	nove	nueve	neuf
10	decem	dieci	diez	dix

Exercise 1.1

1 Who used to speak Latin? (1)

2 Name the area of Italy where the city of Rome was situated. (1)

3 What is the name of the river on which Rome stands? (1)

4 What name is given to the large area which was eventually controlled by Rome? (1)

5 What name is given to languages such as French and Italian which are closely connected with Latin? (1)

Total: 5

Exercise 1.2

Copy and complete the Latin words to arrive at a translation of the English.

Example

He is walking. ambul......... . Answer: ambul..at.........

Note: (sing.) is the abbreviation for singular and (pl.) for plural.

1 He loves.   am......... .

2 You (sing.) walk.   ambul......... .

3 They shout.   clam......... .

4 We enter.   intr......... .

5 They prepare.   par......... .

6 They walk.   ambul......... .

7 We are fighting.   pugn......... .

8 I am hurrying.   festin......... .

9 He carries.   port......... .

10 You (pl.) live.   habit......... .

11 She is working.   labor......... .

12 We are singing.   cant......... .

13 You (sing.) fight.   pugn.........

14 She is walking.   ambul......... .

15 They carry.   port......... .

16 I carry.   port......... .

17 You (sing.) shout.   clam......... .

18 They live.   habit......... .

19 She loves.   am......... .

20 He is working.   labor......... .

21 They are hurrying.   festin......... .

22 They hurry.   festin......... .

23 She is fighting.   pugn......... .

24 We are loving.   am......... .

25 They work.   labor......... .

26 I live.   habit......... .

27 They sing.   cant......... .

28 He enters.   intr......... .

29 You (pl.) enter.   intr......... .

30 You (pl.) carry.   port......... .

31 I am walking.   ambul......... .

32 He shouts.   clam......... .

33 You (pl.) prepare.   par......... .

34 They fight.   pugn......... .

35 They are loving.   am......... .

36 We are working.   labor......... .

37 You (pl.) sing.   cant......... .

38 They enter.   intr......... .

39 He hurries.   festin......... .

40 We live.   habit......... .

1 mark for each question. Total: 40

Exercise 1.3

Translate the following into Latin:

1 You (sing.) love.
2 We enter.
3 They carry.
4 He lives.
5 You (pl.) shout.
6 We walk.
7 I walk.
8 They work.

9 She prepares.
10 You (sing.) hurry.
11 They are fighting.
12 We sing.
13 I am working.
14 They sing.
15 You (pl.) are fighting.

1 mark for each question. Total: 15

Exercise 1.4

Translate the following into Latin:

1 We love.
2 You (sing.) live.
3 We are working.
4 We sing.
5 He walks.
6 You (sing.) are shouting.
7 We carry.
8 You (pl.) enter.

9 I am singing.
10 We fight.
11 They are preparing.
12 They hurry.
13 You (sing.) prepare.
14 You (pl.) carry.
15 She hurries.

1 mark for each question. Total: 15

Exercise 1.5

Translate the following verb forms into English:

1 porto.

2 intrat.

3 habitant.

4 paro.

5 amas.

6 habitatis.

7 intras.

8 laboro.

9 cantamus.

10 laboras.

11 cantatis.

12 habitamus.

13 clamat.

14 festinant.

15 clamas.

16 paratis.

17 habitat.

18 pugnamus.

19 laborant.

20 ambulant.

21 habitas.

22 paramus.

23 laboratis.

24 pugnas.

25 habito.

26 parat.

27 pugnat.

28 festinatis.

29 ambulatis.

30 festinamus.

31 portant.

32 intramus.

33 laborat.

34 paras.

35 pugnatis.

36 portatis.

37 intratis.

38 festino.

39 cantant.

40 portamus.

41 intrant.

42 festinas.

43 clamo.

44 laboramus.

45 parant.

46 portat.

47 ambulo.

48 festinat.

49 ambulas.

50 portas.

1 mark for each question. Total: 50

→ The persons

Exercise 1.6

Write the correct answers:

Example
portatis is the *2nd* person *plural* of porto.

1 cantant is the... person ... of canto.

2 pugnat is the ... person ... of pugno.

3 habitatis is the ... person ... of habito.

4 festinas is the ... person ... of festino.

5 ambulamus is the ... person ... of ambulo.

6 portant is the ... person ... of porto.

7 paras is the ... person ... of paro.

8 intratis is the ... person ... of intro.

9 clamat is the ... person ... of clamo.

10 laborant is the ... person ... of laboro.

2 marks for each question. Total: 20

Exercise 1.7

Write the correct answers:

1 laboratis is the ... person ... of laboro.

2 cantas is the ... person ... of canto.

3 clamant is the ... person ... of clamo.

4 pugnamus is the ... person ... of pugno.

5 intrat is the ... person ... of intro.

6 habitat is the ... person ... of habito.

7 parant is the ... person ... of paro.

8 festinatis is the ... person ... of festino.

9 portas is the ... person ... of porto.

10 ambulat is the ... person ... of ambulo.

2 marks for each question. Total: 20

Exercise 1.8

Give the following:

1 The 2nd person singular of canto.

2 The 2nd person plural of canto.

3 The 1st person plural of laboro.

4 The 3rd person plural of clamo.

5 The 3rd person singular of ambulo.

6 The 2nd person singular of **porto**.

7 The 1st person plural of **festino**.

8 The 3rd person plural of **paro**.

9 The 2nd person plural of **habito**.

10 The 3rd person singular of **intro**.

1 mark for each question. Total: 10

→ Hidden subjects in English

Sometimes in English the subject (or doer) of a verb appears to be left out. For example, the sentence:

He is walking and singing actually means *He is walking and* **he** *is singing* (it is the same person doing both actions).

Similarly:

We are shouting and fighting actually means *We are shouting and* **we** *are fighting* (**we** are doing both actions).

Example

I am shouting and singing. = I am shouting and I am singing.
= clamo et canto.

Exercise 1.9

Translate the following into Latin:

1 You (sing.) are walking and singing.

2 They are shouting and working.

3 I am singing and hurrying.

4 They live and fight.

5 We work and prepare.

6 They are singing and shouting.

7 You (pl.) enter and shout.

8 He is shouting and singing.

9 They live and work.

10 We are shouting and hurrying.

2 marks for each question. Total: 20

Exercise 1.10

Translate the following into English:

1 habitamus et laboramus.

2 clamant et pugnant.

3 ambulas et clamas.

4 ambulatis et cantatis.

5 festinant et parant.

6 canto et clamo.

7 clamat et cantat.

8 intramus et paramus.

9 pugnas et habitas.

10 cantant et clamant.

2 marks for each question. Total: 20

Exercise 2.1

Complete the translation of the English sentences into Latin by adding the correct letters to the end of the Latin verbs below. Don't forget the -a of the stem.

> **Remember:** The he, she, it ending is   **-t**
>
> The they ending is   **-nt**

1 Marcus is singing.   Marcus cant.......... .

2 Marcus and Sextus are singing.   Marcus et Sextus cant.......... .

3 Aurelia is fighting.   Aurelia pugn.......... .

4 Flavia is working.   Flavia labor.......... .

5 Julia and Flavia are hurrying.   Julia et Flavia festin.......... .

6 Marcus is shouting.   Marcus clam.......... .

7 Sextus and Flavia fight.   Sextus et Flavia pugn.......... .

8 Aurelia is entering.   Aurelia intr.......... .

9 Cornelius and Publius are shouting.   Cornelius et Publius clam.......... .

10 Valeria is hurrying.   Valeria festin.......... .

1 mark for each question. Total: 10

Exercise 2.2

Translate the following into English:

1 Marcus festinat.

2 Flavia clamat.

3 Valeria cantat.

4 Sextus ambulat.

5 Aurelia laborat.

6 Iulia laborat.

7 Aurelia et Iulia laborant.

8 Cornelius pugnat.

9 Publius pugnat.

10 Cornelius et Publius pugnant.

11 Flavia et Iulia intrant.

12 Marcus laborat.

13 Iulia cantat.

14 Cornelius et Publius ambulant.

15 Valeria ambulat.

1 mark for each question. Total: 15

Exercise 2.3

Translate the following into Latin:

1 Marcus is fighting.

2 Sextus is fighting.

3 Marcus and Sextus are fighting.

4 Flavia is working.

5 Aurelia is working.

6 Flavia and Aurelia are working.

7 Cornelius and Publius are shouting.

8 Julia is hurrying.

9 Aurelia and Flavia are singing.

10 Marcus is walking.

2 marks for each question. Total: 20

→ Present tense – 2nd conjugation

Exercise 2.4

Translate the following into English:

1 video.

2 non video.

3 moneo.

4 Marcus manet.

5 videmus.

6 habent.

7 Aurelia et Valeria manent.

8 non moneo.

9 video et maneo.

10 habemus.

11 monetis.

12 videtis.

13 Iulia manet.

14 non videmus.

15 monemus.

16 manes.

17 Marcus et Sextus non manent.

18 habeo.

19 Flavia videt.

20 Iulia non videt.

Exercise 2.5

Translate the following into Latin:

1 He stays.

2 He does not stay.

3 We warn.

4 You (sing.) see.

5 They stay.

6 She has*.

7 I have.

8 I see and I stay.

9 Marcus is warning (= Marcus warns).

10 Sextus is not warning.

11 Cornelius and Publius are staying.

12 They do not see.

13 You (pl.) warn.

14 He sees.

15 We are seeing.

16 I am not warning.

17 She is warning.

18 You (sing.) do not have.

19 They stay and see.

20 She sees.

*has comes from the verb *I have*

Exercise 2.6

Revise your tables of **amo** and **moneo**, then copy and fill in the empty boxes in these tables – in total there are 30 blanks to fill in.

English	Latin	English	Latin
I shout	clamo	I stay	
you (sing.) shout		you (sing.) stay	
he shouts	clamat	he stays	manet
we shout		we stay	
you (pl.) shout	clamatis	you (pl.) stay	
they shout		they stay	
I have		I am working	
you (sing.) have		you (sing.) are working	laboras
he has		he is working	
we have		we are working	
you (pl.) have		you (pl.) are working	
they have	habent	they are working	
I sing		I see	
you (sing.) sing		you (sing.) see	
he sings		he sees	
we sing		we see	
you (pl.) sing		you (pl.) see	
they sing		they see	

1 mark for each question. Total: 30

Exercise 2.7

Complete the translation of the English sentences into Latin by adding the correct endings to the Latin verbs below. Don't forget the -a or -e of the stem.

> Remember: Some verbs go like **amo**, others go like **moneo**. Check which is which!

1 We love.   am......... .   (1)

2 They see.   vid......... .   (1)

3 You (sing.) have.   hab......... .   (1)

4 I am fighting.   pugn......... .   (1)

5 We are staying and singing.   man......... et cant......... .   (2)

6 Marcus is seeing.   Marcus vid......... .   (1)

7 Aurelia and Valeria are fighting   Aurelia et Valeria
   and shouting   pugn......... et clam......... .   (2)

8 I do not see.   non vid......... .   (1)

9	We walk and see.	ambul......... et vid......... .	(2)
10	We are preparing.	par......... .	(1)
11	We are warning.	mon......... .	(1)
12	You (pl.) do not warn.	non mon......... .	(1)
13	Flavia is singing.	Flavia cant......... .	(1)
14	Sextus is warning.	Sextus mon......... .	(1)
15	I am shouting and fighting.	clam......... et pugn......... .	(2)
16	He is staying.	man......... .	(1)

Total: 20

Exercise 2.8

Revise the present tenses of both **amo** and **moneo** before translating this exercise into Latin:

1	You (sing.) are walking.	(1)
2	We walk and see.	(2)
3	I do not see.	(1)
4	They do not see.	(1)
5	You (pl.) carry.	(1)
6	They stay.	(1)
7	You (sing.) are fighting.	(1)
8	We see and warn.	(2)
9	He is not hurrying.	(1)
10	We do not walk.	(1)
11	You (pl.) are warning.	(1)
12	She is singing.	(1)
13	You (sing.) see.	(1)
14	They do not carry.	(1)
15	We are shouting.	(1)
16	You (pl.) see and stay.	(2)
17	They stay and sing.	(2)
18	Flavia sees and shouts.	(3)
19	I am not staying.	(2)
20	Sextus and Publius stay and fight.	(4)

Total: 30

→ # Revision: the persons

Exercise 2.9

Give the correct Latin form and translate into English:

Example		
The 1st person singular of **amo**	amo	I love

1 The 3rd person singular of **moneo**.

2 The 3rd person singular of **amo**.

3 The 1st person plural of **video**.

4 The 3rd person plural of **clamo**.

5 The 2nd person plural of **maneo**.

6 The 2nd person singular of **habeo**.

7 The 1st person singular of **festino**.

8 The 2nd person singular of **porto**.

9 The 2nd person plural of **paro**.

10 The 3rd person singular of **maneo**.

2 marks for each question. Total: 20

Exercise 2.10

Translate into English and give the person (1st, 2nd or 3rd) and number (singular or plural) in each case:

Example			
amo	I love	1st person	singular

1 amamus.

2 monetis.

3 cantas.

4 videmus.

5 clamatis.

6 manet.

7 ambulant.

8 habeo.

9 pugnat.

10 parant.

3 marks for each question. Total: 30

→ Plural nouns

Exercise 3.1

Write the plural of the following and translate your answer:

Example			
puella	(girl)	puellae	(girls)

1 nauta   sailor

2 agricola   farmer

3 femina   woman

4 insula   island

5 via   .   road

6 filia   daughter

7 sagitta   arrow

8 porta   gate

9 poeta   poet

10 unda   wave

2 marks for each question. Total: 20

→ Nouns and verbs

Exercise 3.2

Translate the following into Latin:

1 The girl is singing. (2)

2 The girls are singing. (2)

3 The sailor sees. (2)

4 The sailors see. (2)

5 Cornelius is working. (2)

6 Cornelius and Flavia are shouting. (3)

7 The sailor is shouting. (2)

8 The women are walking. (2)

9 The daughter is hurrying. (2)

10 The sailors are working. (2)

11 Publius is entering. (2)

12 The daughters are warning. (2)

13 The girl is staying. (2)

14 The girls are staying. (2)

15 Valerius is warning. (2)

16 The girls are staying and singing. (3)

17 The farmer and the daughter are staying. (3)

18 We are warning. (1)

19 You (sing.) have. (1)

20 I see. (1)

Total: 40

Exercise 3.3

Translate the following into English:

1 puella clamat.

2 puellae clamant.

3 femina videt.

4 feminae vident.

5 agricola festinat.

6 Flavia monet.

7 nautae pugnant.

8 filia ambulat.

9 agricolae manent.

10 Cornelius monet.

2 marks for each question. Total: 20

Exercise 3.4

Translate the following into English:

1 filiae cantant. (2)

2 nautae festinant. (2)

3 agricolae monent. (2)

4 femina videt. (2)

5 agricola laborat. (2)

6 agricolae laborant et clamant. (3)

7 puellae clamant et cantant. (3)

8 Publius manet et videt. (3)

9 nauta clamat et pugnat. (3)

10 puellae et feminae festinant. (3)

Total 25

→ Subjects and objects

Exercise 4.1

Copy out these English sentences. Underline the subject (person doing) in **green**; then underline the object (person done to) in **red**.

1 The girl likes the farmer.

2 The farmer likes the girl.

3 The teacher punishes the pupil.

4 The cat is chasing the mouse.

5 The man is looking at the woman.

What do you notice about the word order in this kind of English sentence?

2 marks for each question. Total: 10

> **Remember:** The subject ends in -a.
> The object ends in -am.

Exercise 4.2

Give the Latin object for the following. The Latin subject is given for you:

Example		
girl	puella	puellam

1 farmer	agricola	
2 goddess	dea	
3 sailor	nauta	
4 woman	femina	
5 daughter	filia	

1 mark for each question. Total: 5

> In Latin, the verb (doing word) usually comes at the end of the sentence.

Example

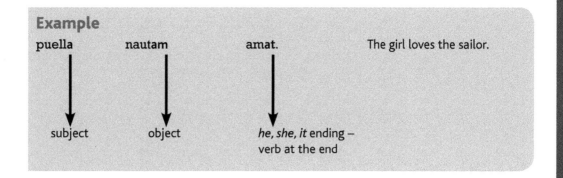

| puella | nautam | amat. | The girl loves the sailor. |

subject   object   *he, she, it* ending –
verb at the end

Exercise 4.3

Translate into English:

1 puella nautam amat.

2 nauta puellam amat.

3 agricola filiam amat.

4 filia agricolam amat.

5 agricola feminam amat.

6 femina agricolam amat.

7 nauta feminam amat.

8 femina nautam non amat.

9 agricola nautam amat.

10 nauta agricolam amat.

3 marks for each question. Total: 30

Exercise 4.4

Translate the following into English:

1 agricola hastam habet.

2 agricola hastam tenet.

3 agricola hastam amat.

4 nauta pecuniam amat.

5 puella reginam laudat.

6 agricola reginam spectat.

7 regina filiam habet.

8 regina filiam amat.

9 agricola filiam vocat.

10 regina deam videt.

3 marks for each question. Total: 30

Chapter 4

Exercise 4.5

Translate the sentences below into Latin. Give **two** answers (answer (a) and answer (b)), using the example here to help you.

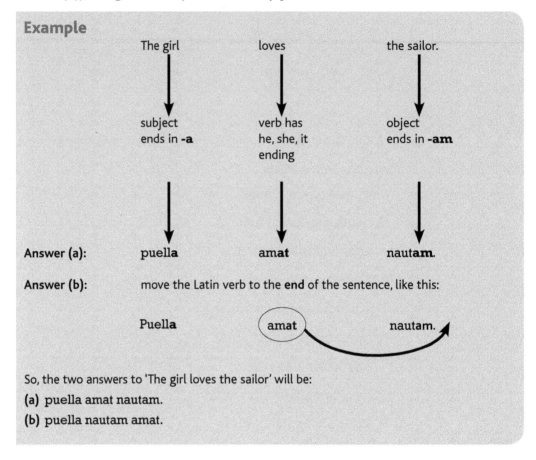

Example

| The girl | loves | the sailor. |

subject ends in **-a** | verb has he, she, it ending | object ends in **-am**

Answer (a):   puella   amat   naut**am**.

Answer (b):   move the Latin verb to the **end** of the sentence, like this:

Puella   *amat*   nautam.

So, the two answers to 'The girl loves the sailor' will be:
(a) puella amat nautam.
(b) puella nautam amat.

1 The girl likes the farmer.

2 The farmer likes the girl.

3 The queen likes money.

4 The woman praises the goddess.

5 The sailor has* a spear.

6 Flavia is looking at the money.

7 The queen has* a daughter.

8 The girl is killing the queen.

9 The goddess warns the queen.

10 The queen loves the sailor.

3 + 1 marks for each question. Total: 40

  *****has** comes from the verb *I have*

Exercise 5.1

Translate the following passage. Line numbers are given on the left. New words are underlined in the text and their meanings given in the margin.

A sailor takes a fancy to Flavia; Flavia takes a fancy to him, too

1 Flavia ambulat. Flavia <u>in via</u> ambulat. Flavia ambulat et cantat.   in via = in the street

    nauta ambulat. nauta <u>in via</u> ambulat. nauta non cantat. nauta Flaviam videt. nauta Flaviam
5 spectat. nauta Flaviam amat.

    Flavia nautam videt. Flavia nautam spectat. Flavia   laeta = happy
    nautam amat. Flavia <u>laeta</u> <u>est</u>. nauta <u>laetus</u> <u>est</u>.   est = is
                                                                                                                   laetus = happy

                                                                                                                   Total 40

Exercise 5.2

1 Give an example of a 1st conjugation verb and write down the line number where it occurs.   (1)

2 Give an example of a 2nd conjugation verb and write down the line number where it occurs.   (1)

3 spectat (line 5). Is the person of this verb 1st, 2nd or 3rd?   (1)

4 videt (line 6). Is the 1st person singular of this verb videmus, vident or video?   (1)

5 Explain the connection between spectat (line 5) and the English word *spectacles*.   (2)

                                                                                                                   Total: 6

➡ Revision: nouns and verbs

Translate the following exercises:

Exercise 5.3

1 cantas.   6 videtis.

2 ridemus.   7 ambulas.

3 tenent.   8 monemus.

4 festinant.   9 non laboro.

5 vocat.   10 habet.

                                                                                                                   1 mark for each question. Total: 10

Exercise 5.4

1 We kill.

2 You (sing.) are holding.

3 They are working.

4 I do not see.

5 You (pl.) have.

6 He is warning.

7 They call.

8 They stay.

9 We are looking at.

10 She is holding.

1 mark for each question. Total: 10

Exercise 5.5

1 regina ridet.

2 puellae rident.

3 agricolae laborant.

4 dea clamat.

5 nauta manet.

2 marks for each question. Total: 10

Exercise 5.6

1 The girl is walking.

2 The girls are walking.

3 Spears kill.

4 The women are laughing.

5 The queen sees.

2 marks for each question. Total: 10

Exercise 5.7

1 agricola hastam tenet.

2 regina filiam habet.

3 nauta puellam videt.

4 puella deam laudat.

5 puellae deam laudant.

3 marks for each question. Total: 15

Exercise 5.8

1 The girl likes the queen.

2 The sailor likes the spear.

3 The goddess warns the woman.

4 The farmer likes money.

5 The farmers like money.

3 marks for each question. Total: 15

Exercise 5.9

1 teneo. (1)

2 pecuniam teneo. (2)

3 videmus. (1)

4 agricolam videmus. (2)

5 necant. (1)

6 feminam necant. (2)

7 spectatis. (1)

8 puellam spectatis. (2)

9 laudat. (1)

10 deam laudat. (2)

Total: 15

Exercise 5.10

1 nauta necat.

2 nautam necat.

3 regina vocat.

4 reginam vocat.

5 filia videt.

6 filiam videt.

7 puella ridet.

8 pecuniam portat.

9 hastam amamus.

10 pecuniam amant.

2 marks for each question. Total: 20

Exercise 5.11

1 I like money.

2 We see the queen.

3 They are carrying the girl.

4 You (sing.) call the goddess.

5 They are not laughing.

6 He is holding a spear.

7 You (pl.) like the sailor.

8 She is killing the farmer.

9 I praise the woman.

10 We see the daughter.

2 marks for each question. Total: 20

➔ cur? and quod

Chapter 5

Exercise 5.12

Translate the following into English:

1	Marcus ridet.	(1)
2	cur Marcus ridet?	(2)
3	Marcus ridet quod non laborat.	(3)
4	nauta hastam habet.	(3)
5	cur nauta hastam habet?	(4)
6	nauta hastam habet quod pugnat.	(5)
7	puella nautam amat.	(3)
8	cur puella nautam amat?	(4)
9	puella nautam amat quod nauta pecuniam habet.	(7)
10	femina agricolam timet.	(3)
11	cur femina agricolam timet?	(4)
12	femina agricolam timet quod hastam portat.	(6)

Total: 45

Exercise 5.13

Translate the following into English:

1	Iulia Flaviam timet.	(3)
2	cur Iulia Flaviam timet?	(4)
3	Iulia Flaviam timet quod Flavia Iuliam terret.	(7)
4	agricola reginam necat.	(3)
5	cur agricola reginam necat?	(4)
6	agricola reginam necat quod reginam non amat.	(7)
7	Publius puellam terret.	(3)
8	cur Publius puellam terret?	(4)
9	Publius puellam terret quod puellam non amat.	(7)
10	puellae agricolam spectant.	(3)
11	cur puellae agricolam spectant?	(4)
12	puellae agricolam spectant quod agricolam amant.	(6)

Total: 55

→ Singulars and plurals

Exercise 5.14

Put into the plural and translate your answer:

1 puella

2 femina

3 regina

4 agricola

5 nauta

2 marks for each question. Total: 10

Exercise 5.15

Put into the singular and translate your answer:

1 filiae

2 deae

3 hastae

4 nautae

5 puellae

2 marks for each question. Total: 10

Exercise 5.16

Put these singular verbs into the plural and translate your answer:

Example		
singular verb	plural verb	translation of plural verb
amo	amamus	we love

1 vides.

2 clamat.

3 habitat.

4 maneo.

5 necas.

2 marks for each question. Total: 10

Exercise 5.17

Put these plural verbs into the singular and translate your answer:

Example		
plural verb	singular verb	translation of singular verb
spectant	spectat	he looks at

1 cantamus.

2 necatis.

3 habemus.

4 monent.

5 terretis.

2 marks for each question. Total: 10

Exercise 5.18

Put into the plural and translate your answer:

Example

regina pugnat. (The queen is fighting.)   reginae pugnant. (The queens are fighting.)

1 puella laborat.   (4)

2 puella videt.   (4)

3 femina monet.   (4)

4 femina festinat.   (4)

5 nauta intrat.   (4)

Total: 20

Exercise 5.19

Put into the singular and translate your answer:

Example

puellae ambulant. (The girls are walking.)   puella ambulat. (The girl is walking.)

1 hastae necant.   (4)

2 reginae rident.   (4)

3 nautae manent.   (4)

4 deae vocant.   (4)

5 filiae manent.   (4)

Total: 20

Exercise 5.20

Put into the plural and translate your answer:

1 puella ambulat.   (4)

2 hasta necat.   (4)

3 dea ridet.   (4)

4 nauta festinat.   (4)

5 filia manet.   (4)

Total: 20

Exercise 5.21

Put into the singular and translate your answer:

1   feminae cantant. (4)

2   reginae vident. (4)

3   puellae rident. (4)

4   agricolae necant. (4)

5   nautae portant. (4)

Total: 20

Exercise 6.1

Translate the following passage. Line numbers are given on the left. New words are underlined in the text and their meanings given in the margin.

Flavia invites Marcus to her place

1 Marcus est nauta. in via ambulat. Flavia est
puella. Flavia quoque in via ambulat. Flavia
festinat. ad villam festinat.

Marcus Flaviam videt. Flaviam amat. ad
5 Flaviam festinat. Flaviam rogat: 'cur festinas,
puella?'

Flavia nautam spectat. nautam amat.
respondet: 'salve, nauta. ego sum Flavia. festino
quod cenam paro.'

10 Marcus Flaviam rogat: 'ubi habitas, Flavia?

Flavia respondet: 'in villa habito. cenam in villa
paro.'

Flavia Marcum ad cenam invitat. Marcus
laetus est. 'euge!' respondet.

15 Flavia et Marcus ad villam festinant.

Margin notes:

est = is
in via = in the street
quoque = also
ad = towards
villa = villa
rogat = he asks

respondet = she/he replies
salve = hello
ego sum = I am
cena = dinner
ubi ...? = where ...?

invitat = invites
laetus = happy
euge! = great!

Total 66

Exercise 6.2

1 ambulat (line 1). Is the person of this verb 1st, 2nd or 3rd? (1)

2 videt (line 4). Is the Latin subject of this Marcus or Flaviam? (1)

3 festinant (line 15). Is the number of this verb singular or plural? (1)

4 This question tests your knowledge of the origins of English words. Complete
the table below. One example has been completed for you. (2)

Latin word from passage	Meaning of the Latin word	An English word that comes from the Latin word
spectat (line 7)	he watches	spectator
habitas (line 10)		

Total: 5

→ Plural objects in -as

Exercise 6.3

Translate the following into English:

1 puella nautam monet.

2 puella nautas monet.

3 puellae nautam monent.

4 puellae nautas monent.

5 femina agricolam amat.

6 femina agricolas amat.

7 feminae agricolam amant.

8 feminae agricolas amant.

9 puellae cenam amant.

10 agricola puellas spectat.

3 marks for each question. Total: 30

Exercise 6.4

Translate the following into English:

1 agricolae puellam spectant.

2 femina cenam parat.

3 regina deam laudat.

4 feminae puellas vocant.

5 nauta villam habet.

6 puellae hastas non portant.

7 feminae agricolas timent.

8 nauta pecuniam videt.

9 agricolae deam non laudant.

10 feminae cenam parant.

3 marks for each question. Total: 30

Exercise 6.5

Translate the following into Latin:

1 The girl likes the farmer.

2 The girls like the farmer.

3 The girl likes the farmers.

4 The girls like the farmers.

   5 The farmers are looking at the girl.

   6 The farmers are looking at the girls.

   7 The queen has a villa.

   8 The sailor is looking at the villas.

   9 The women see the sailors.

   10 The sailors see the women.

3 marks for each question. Total: 30

Exercise 6.6

Translate the following into Latin:

   1 The sailors are looking at the girls.

   2 The girl is preparing dinner.

   3 Women like villas.

   4 The goddess likes the villa.

   5 The queen is calling the sailors.

   6 The girls are praising the goddess.

   7 Women fear sailors.

   8 Sailors frighten women.

   9 The goddess calls the queen.

   10 The girls are looking at the sailors.

3 marks for each question. Total: 30

Exercise 6.7

Translate the following into English:

   1 pecuniam amo.

   2 puellas spectamus.

   3 villam vides.

   4 cenam parant.

   5 puella manet.

   6 villas spectant.

   7 villam intramus.

   8 agricolam vides.

   9 hastam moveo.

   10 nautae non pugnant.

2 marks for each question. Total: 20

Chapter 6

Exercise 6.8

Translate the following into English:

1 agricolam vocas.

2 cenam habemus.

3 agricolae spectant.

4 filiam habeo.

5 puellas amant.

6 deam laudamus.

7 villam video.

8 feminas amatis.

9 agricolae non laborant.

10 cenam laudamus.

2 marks for each question. Total: 20

Exercise 6.9

Translate the following into Latin:

1 I like girls.

2 I like the girl.

3 They are preparing dinner.

4 He has a villa.

5 We are calling the women.

6 We see the farmers.

7 The sailors are fighting.

8 He is moving the spear.

9 They are moving the spears.

10 I praise the goddess.

2 marks for each question. Total: 20

Exercise 6.10

Translate the following into Latin:

1 They are looking at the dinner.

2 You (sing.) like villas.

3 He warns the woman.

4 He warns the women.

5 You (pl.) fear the goddess.

6 They like girls.

7 I have a villa.

8 Girls do not fight.

9 You (sing.) like the farmers.

10 She is preparing dinner.

2 marks for each question. Total: 20

➜ ## Revision: verbs

Exercise 6.11

Give the correct Latin form and translate into English:

Example		
The 2nd person singular of amo	amas	you love

1 The 1st person plural of **porto**.

2 The 1st person singular of **video**.

3 The 2nd person singular of **voco**.

4 The 2nd person plural of **neco**.

5 The 3rd person singular of **laudo**.

6 The 3rd person plural of **teneo**.

7 The 2nd person plural of **terreo**.

8 The 1st person plural of **timeo**.

9 The 2nd person singular of **rogo**.

10 The 3rd person singular of **respondeo**.

2 marks for each question. Total: 20

Exercise 6.12

Translate into English and give the person (1st, 2nd or 3rd) and number (singular or plural) in each case:

Example			
amo	I love	1st person	singular

1 respondemus.

2 rogas.

3 terreo.

4 timetis.

5 laudas.

6 tenent.

7 necat.

8 spectamus.

9 rident.

10 vocas.

3 marks for each question. Total: 30

Exercise 7.1

Translate the following passage. Line numbers are given on the left. New words are underlined in the text and their meanings given in the margin.

Marcus and Flavia share an intimate dinner together

1 Marcus et Flavia <u>ad</u> villam festinant. <u>tandem</u>
villam intrant. <u>quis</u> laborat? Flavia laborat.
cenam parat. cenam <u>bonam</u> parat. <u>dum</u> Flavia
cenam parat, Marcus <u>sedet</u>. <u>vinum</u> <u>bibit</u>.
5 Marcus <u>vinum</u> amat. <u>tandem</u> cena <u>parata</u> <u>est</u>.
Flavia <u>prope</u> Marcum <u>sedet</u>. cenam
<u>consumunt</u> et <u>vinum</u> <u>bibunt</u>. cena <u>bona</u> <u>est</u>. quod
cena <u>bona</u> <u>est</u>, Marcus cenam laudat.

Marcus Flaviam quoque laudat quod cena
10 <u>bona</u> <u>est</u>. 'vinum amo,' <u>inquit</u> Marcus. '<u>vinum</u>
<u>bonum</u> <u>est</u>. cenam amo. cena quoque <u>bona</u>
<u>est</u>.'

Marcus <u>vinum</u> <u>iterum</u> <u>bibit</u>. Flavia Marcum
spectat. 'puella <u>bona</u> <u>es</u>,' <u>inquit</u> Marcus. Flavia
15 non respondet <u>sed</u> ridet. <u>deinde</u> <u>rubet</u>.

ad = to
tandem = finally
quis (+ *verb with a he
ending*) = who?
bonus* = good
dum = while
sedeo (2) = I sit.
bibit = he drinks
vinum = wine
parata = ready
est = is
prope = near
consumunt = they eat
bibunt = they drink
inquit = says
iterum = again
es = you are
sed = but
deinde = then
rubeo (2) = I blush

Total: 85

*The endings on adjectives like **bonus** change depending on which noun they are describing.

Exercise 7.2

1 laborat (line 2). Is the number of this verb singular or plural? (1)

2 bibit (line 4). Is the person of this verb 1st, 2nd or 3rd? (1)

3 laudat (line 9). Is the Latin object of this verb **Marcus** or **cenam**? (1)

4 spectat (line 14). Is the 1st person singular of this **spectatis**, **specto** or **spectant**? (1)

5 This question tests your knowledge of the origins of English words. Complete the table below. One example has been completed for you. (2)

Latin word from passage	Meaning of the Latin word	An English word that comes from the Latin word
amat (line 5)	he loves	amateur
ridet (line 15)		

Total: 6

→ Conjunctions

Note: Do not confuse this word with *conjugation* which means a family of verbs.

A conjunction is a joining word like **sed** *(but)* and **et** *(and)*. Conjunctions are used to join two short sentences into a single, longer one.

Examples	
ridet.	He laughs.
clamat.	He shouts.
ridet **et** clamat.	He laughs **and** shouts.
cantat.	He is singing.
timet.	He is afraid.
cantat **sed** timet.	He is singing **but** he is afraid.

Exercise 7.3

Translate the following into English:

1	agricolae clamant.	(2)
2	agricolae pugnant.	(2)
3	agricolae clamant et pugnant.	(3)
4	sedet.	(1)
5	laborat.	(1)
6	non laborat.	(2)
7	puellae rident.	(2)
8	puellae cantant.	(2)
9	puellae rident et cantant.	(4)
10	non cantant.	(2)
11	timent.	(1)
12	cantant sed timent.	(3)
13	spectamus.	(1)
14	ridemus.	(1)
15	spectamus et ridemus.	(3)

Total: 30

→ sum – present tense

Exercise 7.4

Translate the following into English:

1	puella sum.	(2)
2	femina est.	(2)
3	nauta es.	(2)

4 agricolae sumus. (2)

5 deae estis. (2)

6 puellae sunt. (2)

7 quis es? (2)

8 regina sum. (2)

9 Flavia puella est. (3)

10 Flavia et Iulia nautae non sunt. (6)

Total: 25

Exercise 7.5

Translate the following into Latin:

Beware: The verb *to be* is always followed by a nominative noun, **not** an accusative one.

Example

He is a sailor = **nauta est** (**not nautam est**).

1 I am a farmer. (2)

2 We are women. (2)

3 You (sing.) are the queen. (2)

4 She is Flavia. (2)

5 You (pl.) are sailors. (2)

6 They are girls. (2)

7 He is a farmer. (2)

8 Marcus is a sailor. (3)

9 Marcus and Sextus are sailors. (4)

10 Flavia is not a sailor. (4)

Total: 25

Exercise 7.6

Translate the following into English:

1 Flavia Romana est.

2 Flavia et Iulia Romanae sunt.

3 Marcus Romanus est.

4 Marcus et Sextus Romani sunt.

5 Flavia Graeca non est.

6 Flavia et Iulia Graecae non sunt.

7 Marcus Graecus non est.

8 Marcus et Sextus Graeci non sunt.

9 puella Graeca sum.

10 puellae Graecae sumus.

3 marks for each question. Total: 30

Exercise 7.7

Translate the following into English:

1 nautae Romani sumus. (3)

2 Marcus nauta Romanus est. (3)

3 puella Graeca es. (3)

4 puellae Romanae sunt. (3)

5 Flavia puella Romana est. (3)

6 Flavia et Iulia puellae Romanae sunt. (4)

7 Graeci sumus. (2)

8 Romani non sunt. (3)

9 Flavia femina est. (3)

10 Flavia Graeca non est. (3)

Total: 30

Exercise 7.8

Translate the following into Latin:

1 He is not Roman. (3)

2 She is a Roman. (2)

3 Julia is not Greek. (4)

4 Marcus is not Greek. (4)

5 We are Romans. (2)

6 We are not Greeks. (3)

7 Publius is a Roman. (3)

8 I am a Roman. (2)

9 I am a Roman farmer. (3)

10 Julia is not a Roman. (4)

Total: 30

Exercise 7.9

Translate the following into Latin:

1 Marcus is a Roman. (3)

2 Marcus and Sextus are Romans. (5)

3 Marcus is a Roman sailor. (4)

4 Marcus is not a Greek sailor. (5)

5 We are not Romans. (3)

6 The girl is Roman. (3)

7 She is not a Greek. (3)

8 You (sing.) are a Greek girl. (3)

9 You (pl.) are Greek girls. (3)

10 Publius is a Greek. (3)

Total: 35

(Now try Test 1 at the end of the book.)

Exercise 8.1

Translate the following passage. Line numbers are given on the left. New words are underlined in the text and their meanings given in the margin.

Marcus and Flavia enjoy each other's company

1 Marcus est nauta Romanus. Flavia est puella
Romana. Marcus et Flavia in villa sunt. cenam
consumunt et vinum bibunt. cena bona est.
Marcus cenam amat. vinum quoque bonum
5 est. Marcus vinum quoque amat.

> consumunt = they eat
> vinum = wine
> bibunt = they drink bona/
> bonum = good

Marcus cenam laudat quod cena bona est.
Marcus Flaviam quoque laudat quod Flavia
puella bona est. quod Marcus Flaviam laudat,
Flavia rubet.

> rubeo (2) = I blush

10 Marcus prope Flaviam sedet. Marcus Flaviam
spectat. Marcus Flaviam diu spectat. Flaviam
amat. Flavia prope Marcum sedet. Flavia
Marcum spectat. Flavia Marcum diu spectat.
Marcum amat.

> prope = near
> diu = for a long time

15 tandem Marcus 'te amo, Flavia,' inquit. 'amasne
me, Flavia?' Flavia respondet: 'te quoque amo,
Marce!'

> te = you (*this is an
> accusative ending*)
> ne *turns a sentence into a
> question*
> me = me
> basio (1) = I kiss
> nunc = now

deinde Flavia Marcum basiat. nunc Marcus
rubet. Flaviam amat.

Total: 100

Exercise 8.2

1 sunt (line 2).

   (i) Is the person of this verb 1st, 2nd or 3rd?

   (ii) Is the number of this verb singular or plural?

   (iii) Is the 1st person singular of this verb **sumus, sum** or **es**? (3)

2 et (line 2). Is this word a noun, a conjunction or a verb? (1)

3 basiat (line 18). Is the Latin subject of this verb **Flavia** or **Marcum**? (1)

Total: 5

→ Revision: verbs

Exercise 8.3

Translate the following into Latin:

1 They rule.

2 You (sing.) are leading.

3 She hears.

4 He is sleeping.

5 We do.

6 You (pl.) put.

7 He is running.

8 We run.

9 You (pl.) do.

10 They make.

11 They take.

12 They say.

13 We send.

14 I am coming.

15 You (sing.) rule.

16 They send.

17 They are sleeping.

18 I am making.

19 We are running.

20 You (sing.) say.

21 We are sending.

22 We hear.

23 We are coming.

24 She comes.

25 They are leading.

26 I hear.

27 They put.

28 I am not running.

29 He is taking.

30 You (pl.) sleep.

1 mark for each question. Total: 30

Exercise 8.4

Translate the following into English:

1 mitto.

2 curris.

3 currunt.

4 rego.

5 dormitis.

6 ducitis.

7 mittit.

8 venimus.

9 ducunt.

10 audimus

11 audis.

12 venitis.

13 mittimus.

14 faciunt.

15 capis.

16 audiunt.

17 dormiunt.

18 mittis.

19 capit.

20 facis.

21 regitis.

22 veniunt.

23 ducimus.

24 ponit.

25 regit.

26 audit.

27 ponitis.

28 capimus.

29 currimus.

30 dicit.

Exercise 8.5

Translate the following into English:

1 puella non laborat. dormit. (3)

2 feminae pecuniam capiunt. (3)

3 cur curris, puella? (3)

4 curro quod festino. (3)

5 puella reginam audit. (3)

6 nautae currunt. (2)

7 cur Marcus timet? (3)

8 Marcus timet quod Publius venit. (5)

9 agricola feminam videt. (3)

10 agricola pecuniam capit. (3)

11 agricola currit. (2)

12 Romani veniunt! (2)

13 cur laboratis, nautae? (3)

14 laboramus quod villam facimus. (4)

15 puellae villas amant. (3)

Total: 45

Exercise 8.6

Translate the following into Latin:

1 The farmer hears the goddess. (3)

2 Sailors like money. (3)

3 The Romans are ruling*. (2)

4 The girl is coming. (2)

5 The woman is taking the money. (3)

*Careful! *They are ruling = they rule.*

6 We are making dinner. (2)

7 You (sing.) are taking the money. (2)

8 I hear the farmer. (2)

9 I do not like the dinner. (3)

10 The farmer is leading his* daughter. (3)

Ignore this word when translating into Latin.

Total: 25

→ # The completely useless present tense verb exercises

Here are some Latin verbs you will not be likely to need in the future.

adnuto (1)	I nod to
mico (1)	I quiver
plico (1)	I fold
lugeo (2)	I am in mourning
sorbeo (2)	I sup up
tergeo (2)	I wipe
torreo (2)	I scorch
adolesco (3)	I grow up
ango (3)	I throttle
emungo (3)	I wipe the nose
frendo (3)	I gnash my teeth
molo (3)	I grind
praecutio (3½)	I shake before
fulcio (4)	I prop

Exercise 8.7

Using the vocabulary above, translate these sentences into Latin:

1 We nod to.

2 He wipes his nose.

3 They are scorching.

4 I quiver.

5 She is in mourning.

6 You (sing.) are supping up.

7 They wipe.

8 We are propping.

9 You (pl.) are gnashing your teeth.

10 We grow up.

11 He is shaking before.

12 You (sing.) are throttling.

13 I am folding.

14 They are grinding.

15 They fold.

1 mark for each question. Total: 15

Exercise 8.8

Using the verb list on the previous page, translate these sentences into English.

1 fulcimus.

2 terges.

3 sorbent.

4 praecutis.

5 adolescunt.

6 luget.

7 torremus.

8 frendis.

9 molo.

10 plicatis.

11 micas.

12 angis.

13 emungimus.

14 adnutat.

15 micant.

1 mark for each question. Total: 15

Exercise 8.9

Although these are not very common Latin verbs, they still have links with some English words. What does each of the following English words mean and with which of the above Latin verbs is it connected?

1 implicate

2 lugubrious

3 adolescent

4 fulcrum

5 complicated

6 absorbent

7 torrid

8 detergent

9 molars

10 anxious

2 marks for each question. Total: 20

→ Open questions using -ne

Exercise 8.10

Translate the following into English:

1 curro.

2 currone?

3 mittimus.

4 mittimusne?

5 rident.

6 ridentne?

7 veniunt.

8 veniuntne?

9 regit.

10 regitne?

11 festinatisne?

12 audisne?

13 cantantne?

14 dormitne?

15 venisne?

16 curruntne?

17 timesne?

18 venitne?

19 manetne?

20 laboramusne?

1 mark for each question. Total: 20

Exercise 8.11

Translate the following into English:

1 amasne puellam?

2 spectasne feminam?

3 agricolane laborat?

4 agricolaene laborant?

5 deamne timet?

6 nautaene currunt?

7 reginane ridet?

8 puellaene audiunt?

9 hastamne habes?

10 cenamne paramus?

2 marks for each question. Total: 20

Exercise 8.12

Translate the following into English:

1 estne Flavia nauta?

2 nautane pecuniam habet?

3 puellaene currunt?

4 nautaene puellam amant?

5 mittisne pecuniam?

6 Marcusne Flaviam amat?

7 puellamne amas, nauta?

8 puellaene nautam audiunt?

9 feminaene deam laudant?

10 agricolaene hastas tenent?

3 marks for each question. Total: 30

Exercise 8.13

Translate the following into Latin:

Hint: Translate first as if the sentence is not a question, then add the **-ne** and the question mark!

1 Are you (sing.) listening??

2 Are they sleeping?

3 Am I shouting?

4 Are we working?

5 Is he praising?

6 Are we sitting?

7 Is he afraid?

8 Are they running?

9 Are we leading?

10 Are you (sing.) looking?

1 mark for each question. Total: 10

Exercise 8.14

Translate the following into Latin:

1 Is the girl fighting?

2 Are the girls fighting?

3 Is the sailor running?

4 Are the sailors running?

5 Is the woman coming?

6 Are the girls sleeping?

7 Is the queen laughing?

8 Do queens rule?

9 Is dinner coming?

10 Is Flavia listening?

2 marks for each question. Total: 20

Exercise 8.15

Translate the following into Latin:

1 Is the woman preparing dinner?

2 Do girls like villas?

3 Is Marcus looking at Flavia?

4 Do spears kill sailors?

5 Are the farmers looking at the queen?

6 Is Flavia a sailor?

7 Are the girls Romans?

8 Are the sailors listening to the queen?

9 Does Marcus like the dinner?

10 Do spears kill?

3 marks for each question. Total: 30

9

Exercise 9.1

Translate the following passage. Line numbers are given on the left. New words are underlined in the text and their meanings given in the margin.

Marcus and Flavia express their feelings for each other

1 Marcus rubet. cur Marcus rubet? Marcus
rubet quod Flavia eum basiat.

   rubeo (2) = I blush
   eum = him
   basio (1) = I kiss

   Flavia Marco, 'rubes, Marce,' dicit. 'cur rubes?
rubesne quod te basio?'

   Marco = to Marcus
   te = you (*this is an object/ person done to ending*)

5 Marcus Flaviae respondet: 'Flavia, laetus sum
quod me basias. laetus sum quod me amas.
rubeo quod puellae me non amant. cur me
amas, Flavia? mene amas quod nauta sum?'

   Flaviae = to Flavia
   laetus = happy
   me = me (*this is an object/ person done to ending*)

   Flavia Marco respondet: 'Marce, te non amo
10 quod nauta es. te amo quod pulcher es.
amasne me, Marce?'

   pulcher = handsome

   Marcus 'te' inquit 'amo, Flavia.'

   Flavia rogat: 'cur me amas, Marce? mene amas
quod cenas bonas paro?'

15 'te non amo quod cenas bonas paras, Flavia,'
respondet Flaviae Marcus. 'te amo quod
puella pulchra es.'

   bonas = good

   pulchra = beautiful

   Marcus Flaviam basiat. Flavia non iam rubet.
Flavia Marcum iterum basiat. Marcus non iam
20 rubet. Marcus Flaviam iterum basiat. Marcus et
Flavia laeti sunt.

   iam = now

   laeti = happy

Total: 125

Exercise 9.2

1 basiat (line 2). Is the Latin subject of this verb **Marcus** or **Flavia**? (1)

2 respondet (line 5). Is this a 1st conjugation verb or a 2nd conjugation verb? (1)

3 paras (line 15). Is the Latin object of this verb **cenas** or **Flavia**? (1)

4 sunt (line 21). Is the 1st person singular of this **sum**, **estis** or **sumus**? (1)

5 This question tests your knowledge of the origins of English words.
   Complete the table below. One example has been completed for you.   (2)

Latin word from passage	Meaning of the Latin word	An English word that comes from the Latin word
dicit (line 3)	he says	dictate
respondet (line 16)		

Total: 6

→ Recognising the cases

If you were translating the sentences in the following three exercises into Latin, into which case would you put each of the underlined words?

Exercise 9.3

1 The Queen of <u>Hearts</u> she baked some <u>tarts</u>.

2 The teacher bribed the <u>children</u> with a <u>Mars Bar</u>.

3 <u>We</u> travelled by <u>taxi</u>.

4 <u>Girl</u>, why are you running from the <u>room</u>?

5 Will you do a <u>favour</u> for <u>me</u>?

2 marks for each question. Total: 10

Exercise 9.4

1 The <u>teacher</u> is chasing the <u>boy</u>.   (2)

2 He shouts, '<u>Boy</u>, what are you doing?'   (1)

3 The <u>teacher</u> beats the boy with a <u>stick</u>.   (2)

4 'Why are you beating <u>me</u>, <u>sir</u>?' asks the boy.   (2)

5 The master replies to the <u>boy</u>, 'I am not beating <u>you</u> for fun, boy.
   You are the cause of the <u>trouble</u>.'   (3)

Total: 10

Exercise 9.5

1 The pupil gave an <u>apple</u> to the <u>teacher</u>.

2 'Thank you, <u>Freddie</u>,' the <u>teacher</u> said.

3 '<u>Mum</u> bought the apple for <u>me</u>,' Freddie replied.

4 'I'm giving it to <u>you</u> for a laugh,' <u>the boy</u> added.

5 'Thank you anyway, <u>Freddie</u>,' said the <u>teacher</u>.

2 marks for each question. Total: 10

→ 1st declension: all cases

Exercise 9.6

Translate each of the following using a **single** Latin word:

1 of a farmer

2 girls (object)

3 by road

4 by sailors

5 of women

6 the roads (object)

7 by waters

8 for the girl

9 of the inhabitants

10 for the farmers

11 of water

12 woman (subject)

13 goddess!

14 with anger

15 with an arrow

16 for money

17 of the maidservants

18 for the girls

19 to the girl

20 by land

21 crowds (object)

22 for the maidservant

23 of the poet

24 with dinner

25 inhabitants (subject)

26 of the island

27 of the islands

28 with water

29 by anger

30 with arrows

31 for the inhabitants

32 the island (object)

33 the islands (object)

34 from the crowds

35 for Flavia

36 to the land

37 with poets

38 of the poets

39 of waves

40 for the crowd

1 mark for each question. Total: 40

Exercise 9.7

Translate each of these phrases, using **two** Latin words:

1 The anger of the goddess.

2 The crowd of inhabitants.

3 The inhabitants of the road.

4 The dinner of the farmer.

5 The money of the poet.

6 The villa of the queen.

7 The daughter of the woman.

8 The water of the island.

9 The sailors of the country.

10 The crowds of girls.

2 marks for each question. Total: 20

Exercise 9.8

Translate each of these phrases using **two** Latin words:

1 For the crowd of inhabitants.

2 With the arrows of the sailor.

3 To the inhabitants of the land.

4 For the poets of the country.

5 With the money of the queen.

6 With the spears of the farmers.

7 For the women of the islands.

8 To the queen of the inhabitants.

9 The anger of the crowd.

10 For the inhabitants of the country.

2 marks for each question. Total: 20

Exercise 9.9

Give the form of the noun requested; then translate your answer into English:

Example		
dative singular of **puella**	puellae	to the girl

1 The genitive singular of **femina**.

2 The ablative plural of **agricola**.

3 The dative singular of **filia**.

4 The genitive plural of **nauta**.

5 The dative plural of **puella**.

6 The genitive singular of **aqua**.

7 The dative plural of **turba**.

8 The genitive singular of **poeta**.

9 The genitive plural of **unda**.

10 The genitive singular of **dea**.

11 The ablative singular of **villa**.

12 The ablative plural of **hasta**.

13 The dative singular of **pecunia**.

14 The nominative plural of incola.

15 The genitive singular of ira.

16 The ablative singular of sagitta.

17 The nominative singular of regina.

18 The genitive plural of femina.

19 The nominative plural of cena.

20 The dative singular of dea.

2 marks for each question. Total: 40

Exercise 9.10

Translate the following into English:

1	hasta nautae.	(2)
2	hasta nautae necat.	(3)
3	filia reginae.	(2)
4	filia reginae venit.	(3)
5	ancilla poetae.	(2)
6	ancilla poetae cantat.	(3)
7	filia feminae.	(2)
8	filia feminae timet.	(3)
9	regina insulae.	(2)
10	regina insulae ridet.	(3)

Total: 25

Exercise 9.11

Translate the following into English:

1	turba nautarum venit.	(3)
2	agricolae puellas terrent.	(3)
3	agricolae puellas hastis terrent.	(4)
4	filia agricolae cantat.	(3)
5	filiae agricolae non cantant.	(4)
6	nauta filiam reginae amat.	(4)
7	femina cenam agricolae parat.	(4)
8	cenam agricolis paramus.	(3)
9	nautae incolas sagittis necant.	(4)
10	turbam puellarum videmus.	(3)

Total: 35

Chapter 9

Exercise 9.12

Translate the following into Latin:

1 I give water to the farmer.

2 I give water to the farmers.

3 I show the money to the inhabitant.

4 I show the money to the inhabitants.

5 We are giving spears to the sailors.

3 marks for each question. Total: 15

Exercise 9.13

Translate the following into English:

1	puella pecuniam agricolae dat.	(4)
2	puella pecuniam agricolis dat.	(4)
3	poeta insulam nautae ostendit.	(4)
4	poeta insulam nautis ostendit.	(4)
5	femina aquam poetae dat.	(4)
6	femina aquam poetis dat.	(4)
7	hastam agricolae do.	(3)
8	villam feminae ostendimus.	(3)
9	cenam nautae paras.	(3)
10	sagittas nautis paro.	(3)

Total: 36

Exercise 9.14

Copy the following and add the right endings to arrive at a correct translation of each sentence or phrase:

1 A crowd of girls.

turb........ puell......... .   (2)

2 The arrows of the sailors kill.

sagitt........ naut........ nec........ .   (3)

3 The poet sees a crowd of farmers.

poet........ turb........ agricol........ vid........ .   (4)

4 The daughter of the farmer is singing.

fili........ agricol........ cant........ .   (3)

5 The maidservants are preparing dinner for the queen.

ancill........ cen........ regin........ par........ .   (4)

6   The sailor is killing the farmers with spears.

   naut........ agricol....... hast........ nec........ .   (4)

                                                              Total: 20

Exercise 9.15

Translate the following into Latin:

   1 I am preparing.   (1)
   2 I am preparing dinner.   (2)
   3 I am preparing dinner for the farmer.   (3)
   4 We are giving.   (1)
   5 We are giving money.   (2)
   6 We are giving money to the girls.   (3)
   7 He shows.   (1)
   8 The farmer shows.   (2)
   9 The farmer shows the spears.   (3)
   10 He shows the spears.   (2)

                                                              Total: 20

→ Revision: nouns and verbs

Exercise 9.16

Translate the following into English:

   1 dormimus.   6 ducunt.
   2 sedet.   7 respondet.
   3 mitto.   8 ponitis.
   4 curris.   9 festinamus.
   5 clamas.   10 venis.

                               1 mark for each question. Total: 10

Exercise 9.17

Translate the following into English:

   1 poetae timent.
   2 regina venit.
   3 undas audis.
   4 sagittas habemus.
   5 incolae dormiunt.

                               2 marks for each question. Total: 10

49

Exercise 9.18

Translate the following into English:

1 agricola terram amat.

2 nautae undas non timent.

3 ancillae reginam audiunt.

4 turba puellas terret.

5 poeta pecuniam capit.

3 marks for each question. Total: 15

Exercise 9.19

Translate the following into Latin:

1 I stay.

2 We come.

3 She is afraid.

4 They sleep.

5 They reply.

6 You (sing.) send.

7 I shout.

8 You (pl.) say.

9 He looks at.

10 We put.

1 mark for each question. Total: 10

Exercise 9.20

Translate the following into Latin:

1 The farmers are running.

2 I see the island.

3 I do not like crowds.

4 We hear the queen.

5 The queen is sleeping.

2 marks for each question. Total: 10

Exercise 9.21

Translate the following into Latin:

1 Sailors like water.

2 The maidservant prepares dinner.

3 The girl listens to the poet.

4 The woman looks at the crowd.

5 The queen rules the land.

3 marks for each question. Total: 15

Exercise 9.22

Put into the plural and translate your answer:

1 via

2 villa

3 cena

4 hasta

5 dea

2 marks for each question. Total: 10

Exercise 9.23

Put into the singular and translate your answer:

1 hastae

2 feminae

3 reginae

4 agricolae

5 puellae

2 marks for each question. Total: 10

Exercise 9.24

Put these plural verbs into the singular and translate your answer.

Example		
amamus	amo	I love

1 capiunt.

2 facitis.

3 currimus.

4 respondent.

5 rogatis.

2 marks for each question. Total: 10

Exercise 9.25

Put these singular verbs into the plural and translate your answer.

Example		
amamus	amo	I love

1 venio.

2 dicis.

3 mittit.

4 videt.

5 amas.

2 marks for each question. Total: 10

51

Exercise 9.26

Put into the plural and translate your answer.

1 puella nautam videt.

2 nauta puellam amat.

3 femina cenam parat.

4 agricola reginam audit.

5 filia hastam tenet.

3 + 3 marks for each question. Total: 30

Exercise 9.27

Put into the singular and translate your answer.

1 agricolae filias amant.

2 puellae hastas spectant.

3 feminae deas audiunt.

4 nautae hastas mittunt.

5 feminae filias habent.

3 + 3 marks for each question. Total: 30

Exercise 10.1

Translate the following passage. Line numbers are given on the left. New words are underlined in the text and their meanings given in the margin.

A punch-up in the classroom

1 Sextus et Flavia discipuli sunt. in ludo
laborant. scribunt. Sextus Flaviam non amat.
Flaviam non amat quod puella est. puellas non
amat. Flavia Sextum non amat. Sextum non
5 amat quod puer est. Flavia pueros non amat,
praeter Marcum.

subito Sextus Flaviam pulsat. Sextus puellas
saepe pulsat. Flavia igitur Sextum pulsat.
Sextus Flaviam iterum pulsat. pugnant.
10 magister Sextum et Flaviam videt. 'quid
facitis?' clamat. 'cur pugnatis?' Sextus et Flavia
non iam pugnant. magistrum spectant. 'Sextus
me semper pulsat,' respondet Flavia. 'Flavia me
semper pulsat,' respondet Sextus. magister
15 iratus est. Sextum punit. Sextus flet. magister
Flaviam quoque punit. Flavia quoque flet.
Flavia et Sextus non laeti sunt. magistrum non
amant.

discipulus = pupil
ludus = school
scribo (3) = I write

praeter = except for

subito = suddenly
pulso (1) = I thump
saepe = often
igitur = therefore
magister = teacher
quid = what
me = me (*this is an object/
person done to ending*)
semper = always
iratus = angry
punio (4) = I punish
fleo (2) = I cry
laeti = happy

Total: 100

Exercise 10.2

1 laborant (line 2). Is the number of this verb singular or plural? (1)

2 scribunt (line 2). Is the person of this verb 1st, 2nd or 3rd? (1)

3 Flaviam (line 2). Is the case of this noun nominative, accusative or genitive? (1)

4 puellas (line 3). Give the case of this noun. Why is this case used? (2)

Total: 5

→ 2nd declension nouns

Exercise 10.3

Translate the following into English:

1 amicus currit.

2 amicum habeo.

3 amici pugnant.

4 amicos non habes.

5 gladios habemus.

6 dominum timent.

7 nuntius venit.

8 nuntii veniunt.

9 servus festinat.

10 muros spectas.

2 marks for each question. Total: 20

Exercise 10.4

Translate the following into English:

1 equum habet.

2 equos amamus.

3 servi pugnant.

4 filium habes.

5 deus clamat.

6 dominum timent.

7 nuntius venit.

8 nuntii veniunt.

9 servus festinat.

10 muros spectas.

2 marks for each question. Total: 20

Exercise 10.5

Translate the following into English:

1 dominus servum habet.

2 domini servos habent.

3 socii equos amant.

4 servi cibum parant.

5 servi dominum audiunt.

6 gladius amicum terret.

7 deus gladios non timet.

8 amici ventum timent.

9 dominus nuntium mittit.

10 gladii servos necant.

3 marks for each question. Total: 30

Exercise 10.6

Translate the following into English:

1 socii gladios habent.

2 deus dominum vocat.

3 dominus deum timet.

4 filius dominum audit.

5 servus cibum portat.

6 equi cibum amant.

7 servi amicos non habent.

8 dominus locum amat.

9 socii muros spectant.

10 amici murum spectant.

3 marks for each question. Total: 30

Exercise 10.7

Translate the following into Latin:

1 The slave is hurrying.

2 The slaves are hurrying.

3 The master is coming.

4 The masters are coming.

5 The horses are running.

6 The friend is shouting.

7 The friends are fighting.

8 The horse is sleeping.

9 The son is afraid.

10 The god is not afraid.

2 marks for each question. Total: 20

Exercise 10.8

Translate the following into Latin:

1 I have a sword.

2 I have swords.

3 We see the wall.

4 We see the walls.

5 They like horses.

6 You (pl.) are listening to the messenger. (listen to = hear)

7 We fear the master.

8 You (sing.) are preparing the food.

9 He sees the horses.

10 They praise the slave.

2 marks for each question. Total: 20

Exercise 10.9

Translate the following into Latin:

1 The messenger has a son.

2 The son has a sword.

3 The son likes swords.

4 The winds frighten the horses.

5 The master likes food.

3 marks for each question. Total: 15

Exercise 10.10

Translate the following into Latin:

1 The god frightens the master.

2 The gods like the place.

3 The sword kills the horse.

4 The master has a son.

5 The slaves lead the horses.

3 marks for each question. Total: 15

➜ Recognising the cases

Exercise 10.11

If you were translating these sentences into Latin, into which case would you put each of the underlined words?

1 With a <u>flick</u> of the <u>wrist</u> the <u>batsman</u> hit the <u>ball</u>. (4)

2 From the <u>bat</u> the ball flew into the air. (1)

3 The speed of the <u>ball</u> was amazing. (1)

4 The fielder launched himself from the <u>ground</u>. (1)

5 <u>He</u> caught the <u>ball</u>. 'Howzat, <u>umpire</u>?!' (3)

Total: 10

Exercise 10.12

Make up a mini-story of five sentences. From your five sentences, underline a total of ten nouns and say which case each would be if you were translating the sentences into Latin. There should be at least one example of each of the six cases in your mini-story.

1 mark for each noun and 1 mark for each case. Total: 20

Exercise 10.13

Translate the following into Latin. (Only **one** word is needed each time.)

1 of the slave
2 by the sword
3 by the swords
4 with walls
5 horse (object)
6 friends (subject)
7 with food
8 by messenger
9 of the walls
10 for the son
11 messengers (object)
12 for friends
13 with horses
14 master! (person spoken to)
15 of food
16 slaves! (persons spoken to)
17 by horse
18 son (object)
19 from the wall
20 of horses

1 mark for each question. Total: 20

Exercise 11.1

Translate the following passage. Line numbers are given on the left. New words are underlined in the text and their meanings given in the margin.

Marcus finds Flavia crying

1 Flavia amicum habet. amicus Flaviae Marcus
   est. Marcus amicam habet. amica Marci Flavia
   est.

    Marcus per viam ambulat. Flavia quoque per
5 viam ambulat. ad ludum festinat. flet. flet quod
   Sextus in ludo eam semper pulsat. Sextum
   non amat quod puer malus est.

    Marcus Flaviam videt. 'Flavia,' statim rogat
   Marcus, 'cur fles?' Flavia Marco respondet:
10 'O Marce, fleo quod Sextus in ludo me pulsat.
   deinde magister me punit. vir malus est.
   Sextum numquam punit. Sextum non amo.
   puer malus est.'

    Marcus iratus est quod Flavia flet. Flaviam
15 basiat. Flavia iam laeta est quod Marcus eam
   basiat. ridet. Marcus et Flavia ad ludum
   ambulant. Marcus et Flavia laeti sunt.

amica = girlfriend

per = along
ad = towards
ludus = school
pulso (1) I thump
puer = boy
malus = wicked
statim = immediately
magister = teacher
*me = me (this is an object/
person done to ending)*
vir = man
numquam = never

iratus = angry
basio (1) = I kiss
laetus = happy

Total: 100

Exercise 11.2

1 From the passage, quote the line number and give an example of a
   feminine noun. (1)

2 Flaviae (line 1). Is the case of this noun nominative, accusative or genitive? (1)

3 habet (line 2). Is the person of this verb 1st, 2nd or 3rd? (1)

4 ambulant (line 17). Is the number of this verb singular or plural? (1)

5 This question tests your knowledge of the origins of English words.
   Complete the table below. One example has been completed for you. (2)

Latin word from passage	Meaning of the Latin word	An English word that comes from the Latin word
ridet (line 16)	he laughs	ridiculous
amicum (line 1)		

Total: 6

Exercise 11.3

Copy and add the right endings to arrive at a correct Latin translation of each sentence:

1 The slave likes water.

serv......... aqu......... am......... .

2 The slaves are preparing dinner.

serv......... cen......... par......... .

3 The sailors praise the food.

naut......... cib......... laud......... .

4 Farmers like horses.

agricol......... equ......... am......... .

5 The Greeks are killing the Romans.

Graec......... Roman......... nec......... .

6 The farmer does not have a horse.

agricol......... equ......... non hab......... .

7 The messenger is looking at the man.

nunti......... vir......... spect......... .

8 I have a sword and a spear.

gladi......... et hast......... hab......... .

9 Arrows are frightening the horses.

sagitt......... equ......... terr......... .

10 The masters have villas.

domin......... vill......... hab......... .

3 marks for each question. Total: 30

Exercise 11.4

Add the correct endings to arrive at a correct Latin translation for each sentence:

1 The slave of the farmer is running.

serv......... agricol......... curr......... .   (3)

2 The slaves destroy the land with spears.

serv......... terr......... hast......... del......... .   (4)

3 The farmer gives money to the slaves.

agricol......... pecuni......... serv......... d......... .   (4)

4 The wind is destroying the villa of the master.

vent......... vill......... domin......... del......... .   (4)

5 We are frightening the inhabitants with swords.

    incol......... gladi......... terr......... . (3)

6 The woman is giving money to her friends.

    femin......... pecuni......... amic......... d......... . (4)

7 A crowd of slaves is coming.

    turb......... serv......... ven......... . (3)

8 I am showing the villa to a friend.

    vill......... amic......... ostend......... . (3)

9 They praise the goddess of the island.

    de......... insul......... laud......... . (3)

10 The farmer is destroying the wall with his sword.

    agricol......... mur......... gladi......... del......... . (4)

Total: 35

➜ Prepositions

Exercise 11.5

Translate the following into Latin.

1 on horses

2 on the wall

3 in the villa

4 into the villa

5 across the island

6 with a friend

7 with the sailors

8 near the water

9 away from the wall

10 in the road

2 marks for each question. Total: 20

Exercise 11.6

Translate the following into Latin.

1 towards the water

2 near the place

3 along the road

4 out of the water

5 away from the messengers

6 in the roads

7 to the wall

8 through the water

9 against the allies

10 across the road

2 marks for each question. Total: 20

Exercise 11.7

Translate the underlined phrases into Latin:

1 He is running <u>to the girl</u>.

2 I am giving food <u>to the slave</u>.

3 We are showing the island <u>to the friends</u>.

4 They are hurrying <u>to the island</u>.

5 They are coming <u>to the water</u>.

6 I often give money <u>to the boy</u>.

7 He leads the horse <u>to the wall</u>.

8 We give arrows <u>to the sailors</u>.

9 The girl runs <u>to the friend</u>.

10 The farmers show swords <u>to the Romans</u>.

2 marks for each question. Total: 20

Exercise 11.8

Translate the underlined phrases into Latin:

1 We are playing <u>with friends</u>.

2 He is staying <u>with the girl</u>.

3 They are fighting <u>with swords</u>.

4 I am working <u>with a slave</u>.

5 He rules with <u>anger</u>.

6 We kill the sailor <u>with arrows</u>.

7 The allies are coming <u>with horses</u>.

8 The slave <u>is working with the maidservant</u>.

9 He destroys the wall <u>with a sword</u>.

10 We are fighting <u>with the Romans</u>.

2 marks for each question. Total: 20

Exercise 11.9

Translate the following phrases into Latin:

1 with friends

2 on the horse

3 against the inhabitants

4 with Sextus

5 near the road

6 against the master

7 into the wall

8 in a crowd

9 with slaves

10 with food

2 marks for each question. Total: 20

Exercise 11.10

Translate the following into English:

1 cum Marco

2 ex aqua

3 in via

4 in viam

5 de muro

6 per viam

7 per vias

8 contra Romanos

9 ad insulam

10 ad insulas

2 marks for each question. Total: 20

Exercise 11.11

Translate the following into English:

1 in terra
2 trans viam
3 ab insulis
4 cum sociis
5 prope locum

6 in muro
7 contra ventum
8 in equis
9 cum amico
10 in turba

2 marks for each question. Total: 20

Exercise 11.12

Translate the following into English:

1 prope insulam
2 cum nautis
3 in murum
4 cum feminis
5 contra agricolas

6 in aqua
7 contra Sextum
8 trans aquam
9 ad villam
10 a nuntio

2 marks for each question. Total: 20

Exercise 11.13

Translate the following into English:

1 in muro sedeo.
2 ad villam ambulamus.
3 contra Romanos pugnat.
4 per viam currimus.
5 in villa habitas.

6 prope insulam habitamus.
7 trans viam ambulat.
8 cum amicis cantamus.
9 a villa curris.
10 in villam curris.

3 marks for each question. Total: 30

Exercise 11.14

Translate the following into Latin:

1 I am running in the street.
2 I am running into the street.
3 We come away from the island.
4 They stay in the place.
5 He is sitting on the wall.

6 They are sleeping in the villa.
7 I am fighting against the Greeks.
8 You (sing.) are hurrying across the road.
9 He is singing with a friend.
10 They are walking towards the wall.

3 marks for each question. Total: 30

Exercise 11.15

Translate the following into Latin:

1 on the wall
2 into the wall
3 in the road
4 into the road
5 into the villas

6 in the villas
7 into the place
8 in the place
9 in a crowd
10 into the water

2 marks for each question. Total: 20

Exercise 11.16

Translate the following into English:

1 puer a magistro currit.   (4)

2 puella cum amicis venit.   (4)

3 nautae in muro sedent.   (4)

4 servus in villa habitat.   (4)

5 servi in villis habitant.   (4)

6 vir per vias festinat.   (4)

7 equus ad murum ambulat.   (4)

8 Romani contra Graecos pugnant.   (4)

9 in patria regit.   (3)

10 turba puellarum in viam currit.   (5)

Total: 40

Exercise 11.17

Translate the following into English:

1 puer amicum in via videt.   (5)

2 puellae in equis sedent.   (4)

3 Marcus et Flavia per viam ambulant.   (6)

4 servus aquam in villam portat.   (4)

5 ancilla cenam in villa parat.   (5)

6 equum ex aqua ducit.   (4)

7 agricolae contra nautas pugnant.   (4)

8 nautae ab insula currunt.   (4)

9 pueri prope magistrum laborant.   (4)

10 agricola nuntium ad amicum mittit.   (5)

Total: 45

Exercise 11.18

Translate the following into Latin:

1 The slaves run into the villa.

2 The allies are fighting against friends.

3 The girl is sitting on the horse.

4 The crowd hurries through the street.

5 The crowds hurry through the streets.

4 marks for each question. Total: 20

Exercise 11.19

Translate the following into Latin:

1 The teacher is writing on the island. (4)

2 The slaves carry the food across the road. (5)

3 The man puts the money near the wall. (5)

4 The master sends a slave to the place. (5)

5 The teachers send the maidservants out of the villa. (5)

Total: 24

→ Revision: verbs

Exercise 11.20

Give the correct Latin form and translate into English:

1 The 1st person plural of **punio**.

2 The 3rd person plural of **do**.

3 The 1st person singular of **dico**.

4 The 3rd person singular of **audio**.

5 The 2nd person singular of **duco**.

6 The 3rd person plural of **deleo**.

7 The 3rd person singular of **mitto**.

8 The 3rd person plural of **fleo**.

9 The 2nd person plural of **sedeo**.

10 The 3rd person singular of **scribo**.

2 marks for each question. Total: 20

Exercise 11.21

Translate into English and give the person and number in each case:

1 delemus.

2 ponis.

3 puniunt.

4 facitis.

5 scribis.

6 venio.

7 flet.

8 dormimus.

9 damus.

10 ostenditis.

3 marks for each question. Total: 30

(Now try Test 2 at the back of the book.)

Exercise 12.1

Translate the following passage. Line numbers are given on the left. New words are underlined in the text and their meanings given in the margin.

Marcus thumps Sextus

1   Flavia cum Marco ad <u>ludum</u> ambulat.
    Flavia Marcum amat. amicus <u>bonus</u> est. Flavia
    Sextum non amat. puer <u>malus</u> est. iam ad
    <u>ludum</u> <u>appropinquant</u>. <u>multi</u> <u>discipuli</u> prope
5   <u>ludum</u> <u>ludunt</u>. Marcus Sextum non videt.
    <u>ludum</u> intrat.

    <u>ibi</u> pueri laborant. <u>libros</u> <u>legunt</u> et scribunt.
    magister <u>tamen</u> in <u>ludo</u> non <u>adest</u>. Marcus
    pueros spectat. Sextum videt. ridet. ad
10 Sextum currit. Sextum <u>pulsat</u>. Sextum iterum
    <u>iterumque</u> <u>pulsat</u>. '<u>desiste</u>!' clamat Sextus. 'cur
    <u>me</u> <u>pulsas</u>?' Marcus <u>desistit</u>. '<u>te</u> <u>pulso</u> quod <u>tu</u>
    Flaviam semper <u>pulsas</u>,' respondet Marcus.
    'Flavia <u>amica</u> <u>mea</u> est. <u>tu</u> puer <u>malus</u> es,
15 Sexte!' Marcus Sextum iterum <u>pulsat</u>, deinde
    <u>discedit</u>. Sextus non <u>laetus</u> est. fiet. Marcus
    puer <u>malus</u> est.

ludus = school
bonus = good
malus = wicked
appropinquo (1) = I approach
multi = many
discipulus = pupil
ludo (3) = I play
ibi = there
liber (like ager) = book
lego (3) = I read
tamen = however
adsum = I am present
pulso (1) = I thump
iterumque = and again
desisto (3) = I stop
me = me *(this is an accusative ending)*
te = you *(this is an accusative ending)*
tu = you *(this is a nominative ending)*
amica = girlfriend
mea = my
discedo (3) = I depart
laetus = happy

Total: 100

> **Careful!**
> ludo *(I play)* is a verb and has endings like rego.
> ludus *(school)* is a noun and has endings like servus.

Exercise 12.2

1   From the passage, give an example of (and quote the line number) a preposition followed by a noun in the ablative case.

2   From the passage, give an example of (and quote the line number) a preposition followed by a noun in the accusative case.

3   amicus (line 2). Is the gender of this noun masculine or feminine?

4   Sextum (line 3). Is the case of this noun nominative, accusative or ablative?

5   es (line 14). Is the 1st person singular of this verb est, sumus or sum?

1 mark for each question. Total: 5

Exercise 12.3

Translate the following into English:

1 puer et vir in agro currunt. (6)

2 puer et vir in agrum currunt. (6)

3 magister librum scribit. (3)

4 magister librum pueris scribit. (4)

5 puella puerum non amat. (4)

6 libri pueri in villa sunt. (5)

7 pueri librum magistro dant. (4)

8 equos in agris videmus. (4)

9 turba puerorum ad agrum festinat. (5)

10 vir libros non legit. (4)

Total: 45

➜ ego, tu, nos and vos

Exercise 12.4

Translate the following into English:

1 ego te amo. (3)

2 tune me amas? (3)

3 me amat. (2)

4 vos amamus. (2)

5 nos amant. (2)

6 nos currimus, vos ambulatis. (4)

7 ego rideo, tu fles. (4)

8 vos disceditis, nos manemus. (4)

9 puellae nos spectant. (3)

10 vos pueri Romani estis, nos pueri Graeci sumus. (8)

Total: 35

Exercise 12.5

Translate the following into English:

1 ego puella sum, tu puer es. (6)

2 ego te amo, sed tu me non amas. (8)

3 nos Romani sumus, vos Graeci estis. (6)

4 magister rogat: 'quid vos facitis, pueri? ego laboro.' (8)

5 pueri respondent: 'nos ludimus, magister.' (5)

6 magister clamat: 'ego igitur vos non amo.' (7)

7 pueri clamant: 'cur nos non amas, magister?' (7)

8 magister respondet: 'vos non amo quod non laboratis.' (8)

9 pueri clamant: 'magister, te non audimus. te non amamus.' (9)

10 magister respondet: 'pueri, vos me non amatis, ego vos non amo.' (11)

Total: 75

Exercise 12.6

Translate the following into Latin, using pronouns where possible:

1 I am Marcus, you are Sextus. (6)

2 They like me. (2)

3 We like you (sing.). (3)

4 The teacher does not like us. (4)

5 We do not like the teacher. (4)

6 I am looking at you (pl.). (3)

7 I am warning you (sing.). (3)

8 The master frightens me. (3)

9 The slaves are looking at us. (3)

10 We are afraid of you, sailors. (4)

Total: 35

→ Neuter nouns

Exercise 12.7

Put these phrases into Latin. (Only **one** word is needed each time.)

1 of the war
2 words (object)
3 by the danger
4 shields (subject)
5 for the town
6 of the temples
7 by words
8 with help
9 dangers (object)
10 of the battle
11 with wine
12 with gold
13 from the sky
14 of battles
15 of the shield
16 with a shield
17 from dangers
18 by war
19 towns (subject)
20 with words

1 mark for each question. Total: 20

Exercise 12.8

Translate the following into English:

1 pueri bella amant. (3)

2 templa specto. (2)

3 servus scutum portat. (3)

4 servi scuta portant. (3)

5 feminae aurum amant. (3)

6 agricola caelum spectat. (3)

7 nautae pericula non timent. (4)

8 nauta vinum amat. (3)

9 auxilium non venit. (3)

10 agricolae proelia amant. (3)

Total: 30

Exercise 12.9

Translate the following into English:

1 puella bellum timet. (3)

2 dominus auxilium servis dat. (4)

3 templum in oppido est. (4)

4 pueri verba magistri non audiunt. (5)

5 puellae in templis non ludunt. (5)

6 regina gladium habet. (3)

7 magister puellas verbis terret. (4)

8 nautae in proeliis saepe pugnant. (5)

9 Romani oppidum capiunt. (3)

10 oppidum auxilio Graecorum capiunt. (4)

Total: 40

Exercise 12.10

Translate the following into Latin:

1 The farmers are preparing war. (3)

2 Women do not like wars. (4)

3 The girl likes gold. (3)

4 We hear the words. (2)

5 The slave is carrying wine. (3)

6 I am watching the sky. (2)

7 We like the town. (2)

8 The man sees the danger. (3)

9 The allies have shields. (3)

10 The sailor fears battles and wars. (5)

Total: 30

Exercise 12.11

Translate the following into Latin:

1 We live in a town. (3)

2 We are carrying gold into the temple. (4)

3 The girls are running out of danger. (4)

4 The Greeks are fighting against the Romans. (4)

5 The slave likes the wine of the master. (4)

6 The messengers are sleeping in the temple. (4)

7 The shields of the Romans frighten the girls. (4)

8 The sailors look at the temples of the town. (4)

9 I see danger in the battle. (4)

10 Slaves are killing friends in the war. (5)

Total: 40

→ Revision: 1st and 2nd declension nouns

The following nouns are used in the exercises below:

like puella	like dominus	like puer	like magister	like bellum
hasta (spear)	amicus (friend)	puer (boy)	ager (field)	bellum (war)
nauta (sailor)	cibus (food)			oppidum (town)
pecunia (money)	dominus (master)			periculum (danger)
puella (girl)	equus (horse)			templum (temple)
via (road)	gladius (sword)			vinum (wine)
	murus (wall)			
	servus (slave)			

Exercise 12.12

Give the following:

1 The nominative plural of **nauta**.

2 The genitive singular of **servus**.

3 The ablative plural of **ager**.

4 The dative singular of **vinum**.

5 The vocative singular of **amicus**.

6 The accusative plural of **templum**.

7 The genitive plural of **dominus**.

8 The ablative singular of **gladius**.

9 The genitive singular of **pecunia**.

10 The accusative plural of **bellum**.

11 The ablative plural of puer.

12 The genitive plural of via.

13 The dative singular of hasta.

14 The ablative plural of murus.

15 The genitive singular of equus.

16 The nominative plural of oppidum.

17 The ablative singular of periculum.

18 The ablative singular of cibus.

19 The accusative singular of cibus.

20 The accusative plural of hasta.

1 mark for each question. Total: 20

Exercise 12.13

Translate the following into Latin. (Only **one** word is needed each time.)

1 by the road

2 the walls

3 of the girls

4 of the danger

5 of the dangers

6 with a sword

7 with towns

8 to the horse

9 O, girl!

10 to the friend

11 by food

12 of the wall

13 for the boy

14 by spears

15 temples

16 by wars

17 of the masters

18 from danger

19 to the girl

20 for the money

1 mark for each question. Total: 20

Exercise 12.14

Translate **exactly**. (There may be more than one right answer – but put only one!)

1 viae

2 hastarum

3 muri

4 cibo

5 verbis

6 oppida

7 gladiis

8 amicorum

9 vino

10 agri

11 servis

12 nautae

13 pueris

14 bella

15 templum

16 amico

17 oppidis

18 vini

19 agrorum

20 equo

1 mark for each question. Total: 20

Exercise 13.1

Translate the following passage. Line numbers are given on the left. New words are underlined in the text and their meanings given in the margin.

Marcus and Flavia encounter some drunken sailors

1 Marcus et Flavia in oppido sunt. <u>tabernam</u> intrant. <u>ubi</u> <u>tabernam</u> intrant, sedent. cibum <u>consumunt</u> et vinum <u>bibunt</u>. in <u>taberna</u> <u>diu</u> manent. cibus <u>bonus</u> est. Flavia cibum amat.

5 vinum <u>bonum</u> est. Marcus et Flavia <u>laeti</u> sunt.

<u>quattuor</u> nautae quoque in <u>taberna</u> adsunt. prope Marcum et Flaviam <u>stant</u>. nautae, quod vinum <u>bonum</u> est, <u>multum</u> <u>bibunt</u>. <u>mox</u> igitur <u>ebrii</u> sunt. Flavia nautas <u>ebrios</u> spectat. nautas

10 timet. Marco <u>itaque</u>, 'Marce,' inquit, 'nautae <u>ebrii</u> sunt. <u>perterrita</u> sum. <u>discedere</u> cupio.' Marcus nautas spectat. <u>ubi</u> <u>eos</u> videt, <u>iratus</u> est. Marcus et Flavia e <u>taberna</u> ambulant. <u>quattuor</u> nautae quoque e <u>taberna</u> ambulant.

taberna = pub
ubi = when
consumo (3) = I eat
bibo (3) = I drink
diu = for a long time
bonus/bonum = good
laeti = happy
quattuor = four
sto (1) = I stand
multum = a lot
mox = soon
ebrii = drunk
itaque = and so, therefore
perterrita = frightened
discedere = to depart
cupio (3½) = I want
eos = them
iratus = angry

Total: 85

Exercise 13.2

1 oppido (line 1). In which case is this noun? Why is this case used? (2)

2 vinum (line 3). Is the gender of this noun masculine, feminine or neuter? (1)

3 amat (line 4). Give the Latin subject and Latin object of this verb. (2)

Total: 5

→ Adjectives

Exercise 13.3

Translate the following into English:

1 puer bonus.

2 puella bona.

3 vinum bonum.

4 servi laeti.

5 multae feminae.

6 templum magnum.

7 templa magna.

8 agricola iratus.

9 villa parva.

10 periculum magnum.

11 multa pericula.

12 gladius bonus.

13 gladii boni.

14 equus fessus.

15 muri magni.

16 verba mala.

17 amici perterriti.

18 servus fessus.

19 dominus saevus.

20 dea irata.

21 equi fessi.

22 bella saeva.

23 multae hastae.

24 magister saevus.

25 murus magnus.

26 vir bonus.

27 servi irati.

28 templum parvum.

29 insula magna.

30 nauta iratus.

2 marks for each question. Total: 60

Exercise 13.4

Translate the following into Latin:

1 A small girl.

2 Small girls.

3 A tired slave.

4 Tired slaves.

5 A big war.

6 Big wars.

7 A happy slave.

8 Much money.

9 Big shields.

10 The angry master.

11 A good word.

12 Bad food.

13 Savage winds.

14 Big battles.

15 A savage war.

16 An angry goddess.

17 Many dangers.

18 A good man.

19 Good food.

20 A big crowd.

21 A good book.

22 For many slaves.

23 Of angry masters.

24 For the good girl.

25 Tired friends (subject).

26 Many spears (object).

27 Good wine (subject).

28 For the happy slaves.

29 With good words.

30 For a small temple.

2 marks for each question. Total: 60

Exercise 13.5

Translate the following into English:

1 servus cibum bonum parat. (4)

2 puer multas puellas spectat. (4)

3 magister iratus pueros malos monet. (5)

4 puellae Romanae sunt. (3)

5 agricola multos agros habet. (4)

6 sunt* multi equi in agris. (5)

7 multi pueri per viam currunt. (5)

8 nautae fessi in villa dormiunt. (5)

9 puellae malae magistrum bonum audiunt. (5)

10 pueri boni bellum saevum timent. (5)

Total: 45

*est/sunt used at the beginning of a sentence may often best be translated as 'there is/there are'.

Exercise 13.6

Translate the following into English:

1 dominus multam pecuniam servis dat. (5)

2 dominus pecuniam multis servis dat. (5)

3 libros bonos saepe lego. (4)

4 magister librum magnum scribit. (4)

5 pueri sunt laeti quod magister est bonus. (7)

6 pueri fessi in agris magnis ludunt. (6)

7 Romani multa oppida capiunt. (4)

8 multi amici cibum bonum laudant. (5)

9 puer puellam scuto magno terret. (5)

10 puer laetus hastam magnam habet. (5)

Total: 50

Exercise 13.7

Translate the following into English:

1 Romani multos gladios et multas sagittas habent. (7)

2 verba magistri irati non audimus. (5)

3 verba irata magistri non audimus. (5)

4 dominus vinum servis fessis dat. (5)

5 servi laeti vinum in oppido magno bibunt. (7)

6 verba puellarum iratarum pueros terrent. (5)

7 pueri boni multos libros legunt. (5)

8 magister iratus est quod pueri boni non sunt. (8)

9 dominus multas hastas amicis bonis dat. (6)

10 pueri cum amicis bonis in agris ludunt. (7)

Total: 60

Exercise 13.8

Translate the following into English:

1 magister aurum pueris bonis dat. (5)

2 femina bona aquam nautae fesso dat. (6)

3 servi cibum pueris bonis parant. (5)

4 puella nautam saevum non amat. (4)

5 agricolae oppida magna non amant. (4)

6 verba magistri irati audiunt. (4)

7 turba feminarum iratarum in oppidum festinat. (6)

8 puella perterrita in villa magna sedet. (6)

9 nauta iratus puellam terret. (4)

10 puella nautam iratum timet. (4)

Total: 48

Exercise 13.9

Translate the following into Latin:

1 The teacher is happy because the boys are good. (7)

2 Good girls fear sailors. (4)

3 The frightened girls are hurrying along the road. (5)

4 Many men look at the big temple. (5)

5 The boy fears the angry master. (4)

Total: 25

Exercise 13.10

Translate the following into Latin:

1 Many men fear the dangers of war.

2 The frightened woman is running out of the temple.

3 Because the boys are running, they are tired.

4 Many slaves have big spears.

5 The master gives water to the tired slave.

5 marks for each question. Total: 25

➜ Revision: nouns and verbs

Exercise 13.11

Put these singular nouns into the plural and translate your answer:

1 insula   4 periculum

2 puer   5 verbum

3 ager

2 marks for each question. Total: 10

Chapter 13

Exercise 13.12

Put these plural nouns into the singular and translate your answer:

1 turbae   4 scuta

2 discipuli   5 vina

3 libri

2 marks for each question. Total: 10

Exercise 13.13

Put these singular verbs into the plural and translate your answer:

1 lego.   4 deles.

2 adest.   5 scribit.

3 discedit.

2 marks for each question. Total: 10

Exercise 13.14

Put these plural verbs into the singular and translate your answer:

1 damus.   4 scribimus.

2 ostendunt.   5 disceditis.

3 fletis.

2 marks for each question. Total: 10

Exercise 13.15

Put into the plural and translate your answer:

1 puer in agro ludit.   (3 + 4)

2 discipulus librum legit.   (3 + 3)

3 vir bellum timet.   (3 + 3)

4 servus scutum habet.   (3 + 3)

5 amicus in proelio pugnat.   (3 + 4)

Total: 32

Exercise 13.16

Put into the singular and translate your answer:

1 puellae vina amant.   (3 + 3)

2 pericula nautas terrent.   (3 + 3)

3 servi in villis laborant.   (3 + 4)

4 nuntii equos ducunt.   (3 + 3)

5 pueri contra puellas pugnant.   (3 + 4)

Total: 32

Exercise 14.1

Translate the following passage. Line numbers are given on the left. New words are underlined in the text and their meanings given in the margin.

The drunken sailors confront Marcus and Flavia; Marcus tells them to get lost

1 Marcus et Flavia e <u>taberna</u> ambulant quod
Flavia <u>quattuor</u> nautas <u>ebrios</u> timet. nautae
quoque e <u>taberna</u> ambulant. '<u>festina</u>, Marce!
<u>eos</u> timeo,' clamat Flavia. <u>festinare</u>
5 <u>constituunt</u>. nautae quoque per viam iam
festinant. '<u>curre</u>, Marce!' clamat Flavia.
currunt. nautae quoque currunt. <u>sic</u> nautae
Marcum et Flaviam mox <u>consequuntur</u>.

nauta <u>primus</u> clamat: 'quid <u>hic</u> facitis?
10 <u>respondete</u>!'

Marcus respondet: '<u>domum</u> ambulamus.'

nauta <u>secundus</u> rogat: 'quis est puella?'

Marcus iratus respondet: 'puella Flavia est.
<u>amica mea</u> est.'

15 nauta <u>tertius</u> clamat: '<u>amica tua</u>? Flavia <u>pulchra</u>
est. tune me amas, Flavia?'

<u>quattuor</u> nautae rident.

'ubi est pecunia?' clamat nauta <u>quartus</u>.

Marcus iam <u>magnopere</u> iratus est. 'pecuniam
20 non habemus. <u>discedite</u>!'

<u>quattuor</u> nautae iam <u>discedunt</u>.

taberna = pub
quattuor = four
ebrius = drunk
festina = hurry!
eos = them
festinare = to hurry
constituo (3) = I decide
curre = run!
sic = thus, in this way
consequuntur = catch up with
primus = first
hic = here
respondete! = answer!
domum = home
secundus = second

amica = girlfriend
meus = my
tertius = third
tuus = your
pulchra = beautiful

quartus = fourth

magnopere = greatly, very
discedite! = push off!
discedo = I depart

Total: 100

Exercise 14.2

1 e (line 1). Is this word a noun, an adverb or a preposition? (1)

2 nautas (line 2). Is the number of this noun singular or plural? (1)

3 facitis (line 9). Is the person of this verb 1st, 2nd or 3rd? (1)

4 rident (line 17). Give the 1st person singular of this verb. (1)

5 This question tests your knowledge of the origins of English words. Complete the table below. One example has been completed for you. (2)

Latin word from passage	Meaning of the Latin word	An English word that comes from the Latin word
timet (line 2)	he fears	timid
clamat (line 4)		

Total: 6

→ Imperatives

Exercise 14.3

Write the following **singular** imperatives in Latin:

1 Hurry!

2 Laugh!

3 Write!

4 Take!

5 Sleep!

6 Listen!

7 Drink!

8 Send!

9 Destroy!

10 Sing!

1 mark for each question. Total: 10

Exercise 14.4

Write the following **plural** imperatives in Latin:

1 Work!

2 Stay!

3 Run!

4 Come!

5 Read!

6 Play!

7 Eat!

8 See!

9 Be!

10 Walk!

1 mark for each question. Total: 10

Exercise 14.5

Translate the following into English:

1 ride, puer! (2)

2 currite, servi! (2)

3 magistrum audite, pueri! (3)

4 veni, amice! (2)

5 oppidum capite, servi! (3)

6 templum spectate, servi! (3)

7 cibum para, serve! (3)

8 pueri, laborate! (2)

9 hic mane, Marce! (3)

10 servum puni, domine!	(3)
11 da puero pecuniam, puella!	(4)
12 pugnate, nautae!	(2)
13 Graecos necate, Romani!	(3)
14 aurum ad dominum mitte!	(4)
15 cenam para, femina!	(3)
16 librum lege, poeta!	(3)
17 amice, da servis cibum!	(4)
18 audi verba mea, domine!	(4)
19 Romanos neca!	(2)
20 venite ad magnum oppidum, amici!	(5)

Total: 60

Exercise 14.6

Translate the following into English:

1 pecuniam cape, serve!	(3)
2 ad oppidum veni, amice!	(4)
3 vinum bibite!	(2)
4 laborate, pueri!	(2)
5 labora, amice!	(2)
6 da pecuniam pueris!	(3)
7 terram rege, regina!	(3)
8 pugna, puer!	(2)
9 specta!	(1)
10 cantate, puellae!	(2)
11 contra Romanos pugnate!	(3)
12 templa spectate, nautae!	(3)
13 vinum bibe, regina!	(3)
14 oppidum capite!	(2)
15 auxilium mitte!	(2)
16 dormite, puellae!	(2)
17 currite, servi!	(2)
18 aurum mitte, regina!	(3)
19 scuta movete, servi!	(3)
20 servos necate, Romani!	(3)

Total: 50

→ Revision: adjectives, nouns and verbs

Translate the following exercises:

Exercise 14.7

1 vinum bibimus.

2 templa spectant.

3 periculum timeo.

4 librum legunt.

5 discipulos punit.

2 marks for each question. Total: 10

Exercise 14.8

1 Help is coming.

2 We like gold.

3 They are eating food.

4 You (pl.) are destroying the temples.

5 She writes books.

2 marks for each question. Total: 10

Exercise 14.9

1 discipuli laeti sunt.

2 liber magnus est.

3 pueri boni sumus.

4 femina perterrita est.

5 magistri irati sunt.

3 marks for each question. Total: 15

Exercise 14.10

1 The horses are tired.

2 I am a good boy.

3 The masters are wicked.

4 The temples are big.

5 The farmer is happy.

3 marks for each question. Total: 15

Exercise 14.11

1 servi in agris laborant.

2 puella te non amat.

3 puer multos amicos habet.

4 bella me non terrent.

5 cum amicis non ludo.

4 marks for each question. Total: 20

Exercise 14.12

1   The teacher does not like us.   (4)

2   He is always angry.   (3)

3   We often play in the road.   (4)

4   We are Romans, but you are Greeks.   (7)

5   Greeks do not like Romans.   (4)

Total: 22

Exercise 14.13

For this exercise you will need to revise:

● The *he, she, it* endings of the present tenses of **amo** and **moneo** (in other words, -at and -et).

● The nominative and accusative singular endings of nouns like **puella** (in other words, -a for subject and -am for object).

Instructions
● Put the Latin subject first in the sentence.
● Put the Latin object second in the sentence.
● Put the verb **at the end**.

1   The farmer has water.

2   The maidservant carries a spear.

3   The crowd kills the farmer. (Careful – *crowd* is a **singular** noun.)

4   The girl praises the goddess.

5   The daughter likes the queen.

6   The woman sees the island.

7   The poet likes the girl.

8   The arrow frightens the poet.

9   The spear kills the sailor.

10 The sailor looks at the women.

3 marks for each question. Total: 30

(Now try Test 3 at the back of the book.)

Exercise 15.1

Translate the following passage. Line numbers are given on the left. New words are underlined in the text and their meanings given in the margin.

Marcus sees off the sailors

1 Marcus et Flavia et quattuor nautae in via
   stant. Marcus magnopere iratus est. nautas
   discedere iubet. nautae, quod Marcum non
   timent, rident. Marco et Flaviae clamant: 'date
5 nobis pecuniam vestram. vinum emere
   cupimus.' Marcus nautas terrere constituit.
   gladium novum habet. gladius bonus et
   validus est. Marcus gladium suum capit et ad
   nautas statim currit. clamat. Flavia perterrita
10 est. Marcus cum nautis pugnat. fortiter
   pugnat. bene pugnat. nautae tamen gladios
   non habent. itaque Marcus nautas mox superat.
   nautae fugiunt. Marcus Flaviam spectat.
   'pecunia nostra tuta est. nos tuti sumus,'
15 inquit. 'te amo, Marce,' respondet Flavia.

discedere = to depart
iubeo (2) = I order
nobis = to us
vester = your
emere = to buy
terrere = to frighten
novus = new
validus = strong
suus = his
fortiter = bravely
bene = well
supero (1) = I overcome
fugio (3½) = I flee
noster = our
tutus = safe

Total: 85

Exercise 15.2

1 Quoting the line number, give from the passage an example of the following:

   (i)   A plural imperative.

   (ii) A cardinal number.

   (iii) An adjective.

   (iv) A neuter noun.

2 cupimus (line 6). Give the person of this verb.

1 mark for each question. Total: 5

➡ Infinitives

Exercise 15.3

Translate the following into English:

1 ludere cupimus.   (2)

2 laborare non cupimus.   (3)

3 festinare cupio.   (2)

4 puellae cantare parant. (3)

5 Marcus pugnare cupit. (3)

6 nautae bibere cupiunt. (3)

7 puer scribere non cupit. (4)

8 discipuli dormire cupiunt. (3)

9 poeta librum legere cupit. (4)

10 domini servos punire semper cupiunt. (5)

Total: 32

Exercise 15.4

Translate the following into English:

1 manere constituit. (2)

2 discedere parant. (2)

3 discipuli laborare constituunt. (3)

4 servus currere constituit. (3)

5 magister discipulos punire constituit. (4)

6 nautae pecuniam capere constituunt. (4)

7 regina terram regere constituit. (4)

8 Romani Graecos superare parant. (4)

9 poeta librum scribere constituit. (4)

10 ancillae cenam parare constituunt. (4)

Total: 34

Exercise 15.5

Translate the following into English:

1 dominus servos laborare iubet. (4)

2 magister discipulos scribere iubet. (4)

3 Marcus nautam discedere iubet. (4)

4 domini servos ludere numquam iubent. (5)

5 agricolas bene pugnare iubet. (4)

6 ego te hic manere iubeo. (5)

7 regina viros hastas parare iubet. (5)

8 dominus servum equum ex agro ducere iubet. (7)

9 dea ancillas templum spectare iubet. (5)

10 dominus servos aquam in villam portare iubet. (7)

Total: 50

Exercise 15.6

Translate the following into Latin:

1 To sing.

2 To see.

3 To put.

4 To come.

5 To order.

6 To decide.

7 To hurry.

8 To play.

9 To write.

10 To be.

1 mark for each question. Total: 10

Exercise 15.7

Translate the following into Latin:

1 To watch.

2 To read.

3 To stay.

4 To fight.

5 To send.

6 To punish.

7 To give.

8 To run.

9 To shout.

10 To laugh.

1 mark for each question. Total: 10

Translate the following four exercises into Latin.

> **Remember:** the main verb goes at the end of the sentence and the infinitive in front of it.

Exercise 15.8

1 We want to play.

2 They decide to work.

3 I want to drink.

4 You (pl.) decide to fight.

5 They want to sing.

2 marks for each question. Total: 10

Exercise 15.9

1 The master decides to hurry. (3)

2 The queen wants to rule the island. (4)

3 The maidservants decide to prepare dinner. (4)

4 Pupils do not want to read books. (5)

5 The sailor decides to punish the slave. (4)

Total: 20

Chapter 15

Exercise 15.10

1 Masters order slaves to work.

2 You (sing.) often order me to stay.

3 The queen orders the slave to sing.

4 Flavia orders Marcus to fight.

5 The masters order the boys to work.

4 marks for each question. Total: 20

Exercise 15.11

1 The man orders the slave to take the money. (5)

2 The woman orders (her) daughter to walk across the road. (6)

3 The queen orders the slaves to prepare food. (5)

4 Marcus orders the farmer to kill the horse. (5)

5 The queen orders the man to send a messenger to the island. (7)

Total: 28

➜ Adjectives in -er

Exercise 15.12

Translate the following into English:

1 in templo sacro sedemus. (4)

2 Marcus nauta notus et clarus est. (6)

3 Flavia misera est quod nautae mali sunt. (7)

4 servi murum aedificant. (3)

5 Romani muros oppugnant. (3)

6 nautae ad insulam navigant. (4)

7 agricolae multas hastas iaciunt. (4)

8 oppidum oppugnate, nautae! (3)

9 viri mali oppidum sacrum hastis et gladiis oppugnant. (8)

10 regina ad terram navigat et oppidum novum aedificat. (8)

Total: 50

Exercise 15.13

For this exercise you will need to revise:

● The *he, she, it* endings of the present tenses of amo and moneo (in other words -at and -et).

● The nominative and accusative singular endings of nouns like puella (in other words -a for subject and -am for object).

Instructions:
- Put the Latin subject first in the sentence.
- Put the Latin object second in the sentence.
- Put the verb **at the end**.

Translate the following into Latin:

1 The woman has water.

2 The sailor carries a spear.

3 The crowd praises the goddess.

4 The goddess praises the daughter.

5 The queen likes the sailor.

6 The woman looks at the island.

7 The girl likes the poet.

8 The arrows frighten the farmers.

9 The spear kills the woman.

10 The woman looks at the sailor.

3 marks for each question. Total: 30

16

(Exercise 16.1)

Translate the following passage. Line numbers are given on the left. New words are underlined in the text and their meanings given in the margin.

Marcus: Flavia's hero

1 Marcus et Flavia tuti erant. Flavia non iam
perterrita erat. etiam Marcum laudabat.
'Marce, tu vir fortis et validus es. ego laeta
sum quod tuti sumus. nautae te timebant.
5 etiam ego te timebam. quod nautae te
timebant, pugnare non cupiebant.'

Marcus Flaviae dixit: 'Flavia, ego quoque laetus
sum quod nos tuti sumus.'

'Marce, veni ad villam meam. cibum habeo.
10 cenam bonam parabo. tu heros meus es.'

'euge!' clamavit Marcus.

Marcus laetus erat. cibum amabat. cenas
Flaviae quoque amabat. Marcus et Flavia igitur
ad villam Flaviae festinaverunt.

erant = were
erat = was
etiam = even
fortis = brave
timebant = (they) were afraid of
timebam = I was afraid of
cupiebant = (they) wanted
dixit = said
parabo = I will prepare
heros = hero
euge! = great!
clamavit = shouted
amabat = he liked
festinaverunt = hurried

Total: 75

(Exercise 16.2)

1 Quoting the line number from the passage, give an example of an infinitive. (1)

2 Quoting the line number from the passage, give an example of an imperative. (1)

3 villam (line 9). In which case is this noun? Why is this case used? (2)

4 habeo (line 9). Is the number of this verb singular or plural? (1)

5 es (line 10).

(i) Is the person of this verb 1st, 2nd or 3rd?

(ii) Is the number of this verb singular or plural?

(iii) Is the 1st person singular of the present tense of this verb est,
    sum or sunt? (3)

6 This question tests your knowledge of the origins of English words.
Complete the table below. One example has been completed for you. (2)

Latin word from passage	Meaning of the Latin word	An English word that comes from the Latin word
validus (line 3)	strong	valid
nautae (line 5)		

Total: 10

→ Imperfect tense

Exercise 16.3

Translate the following into English:

1 vocabamus. (call)
2 laudabat. (praise)
3 ponebam.
4 ludebant. (play)
5 mittebat. (sent)
6 discedebat.
7 capiebat.
8 cupiebant.
9 erat.
10 faciebam.
11 ludebat.
12 ambulabamus.
13 laudabatis.
14 currebat.
15 puniebant.

16 movebat.
17 veniebas. (come)
18 erant.
19 videbamus.
20 bibebant.
21 ambulabat.
22 dormiebam. (sleep)
23 veniebat.
24 ridebas. (laugh)
25 faciebant.
26 audiebatis.
27 capiebamus.
28 portabat. (carry)
29 spectabant. (watch)
30 pugnabamus.

1 mark for each question. Total: 30

Exercise 16.4

Translate the following into Latin:
1st conjugation verbs (like **amo**)

1 She was praising.
2 We were working.
3 I was standing.
4 He used to ask.
5 They were attacking.

6 We were calling.
7 You (sing.) were building.
8 You (pl.) were sailing.
9 They were watching.
10 He used to kill.

1 mark for each question. Total: 10

Exercise 16.5

Translate the following into Latin:
2nd conjugation verbs (like **moneo**)

1 You (sing.) were seeing.
2 We were ordering.

3 They were warning.
4 I was frightening.

87

5 He was answering.

6 I was staying.

7 He was laughing.

8 They were afraid.

9 You (pl.) were holding.

10 We used to have.

1 mark for each question. Total: 10

Exercise 16.6

Translate the following into Latin:
  3rd conjugation verbs (like **rego**)

1 He was leading.

2 They were drinking. bibe

3 I used to read. legere

4 We were sending.

5 He was playing.

6 He was saying.

7 They were deciding.

8 You (pl.) were putting.

9 We were departing.

10 They were running. currere

1 mark for each question. Total: 10

Exercise 16.7

Translate the following into Latin:
  4th conjugation verbs (like **audio**)

1 They were listening. (audire)

2 I was sleeping.

3 He was coming.

4 We were throwing.

5 You (pl.) were hearing.

6 We were taking.

7 You (sing.) were doing.

8 They were coming.

9 She was sleeping.

10 You (sing.) used to take.

1 mark for each question. Total: 10

Exercise 16.8

Translate the following into Latin:
  Mixed grill

1 They were warning.

2 She was drinking.

3 You (pl.) were carrying.

4 We were laughing.

5 They were singing.

6 We were watching.

7 They were staying.

8 He was sending.

9 You (sing.) were running.

10 They were listening.

1 mark for each question. Total: 10

Exercise 16.9

Translate the following into English:

1 hodie ambulo; heri non ambulabam. (5)

2 iam laborat; heri ludebat. (4)

3 discipuli iam laborant; heri non laborabant. (6)

4 hodie bene pugnamus; heri non bene pugnabamus. (7)

5 heri librum legebam; hodie nihil facio. (6)

6 hodie servi celeriter laborant, sed heri lente laborabant. (8)

7 magistrum audi, puer! heri magistrum non audiebas. (7)

8 bene pugnate, Romani! heri non bene pugnabatis. (7)

9 hodie ambulant, sed heri currebant. (5)

10 multi servi per viam festinabant. (5)

Total: 60

Exercise 16.10

Translate the following into English:

1 magister multa verba dicebat. (4)

2 nautae in villa saepe manebant. (5)

3 cur currebas, puer? (3)

4 currebam quod timebam. (3)

5 femina aquam pueris saepe dabat. (5)

6 Romani oppugnabant. hodie non oppugnant. (5)

7 multi servi ex oppido currebant. (5)

8 puellae ludebant sed pueri non ludebant. (6)

9 Romani contra Graecos saepe pugnabant. (5)

10 Graeci Romanos non timebant. (4)

Total: 45

Exercise 16.11

Translate the following into English:

1 Romani oppidum oppugnabant. (3)

2 puer ad villam ambulabat. (4)

3 magister saevus erat. (3)

4 puellas amabam. (2)

5 poeta librum legebat. (3)

6 servi in agris pugnabant. (4)

7 pueri magistrum non audiebant. (4)

8 cur non laborabatis, pueri? (4)

9 per viam ambulabamus. (3)

10 cur ridebas? (2)

Total: 32

Exercise 16.12

Translate the following into English:

1 timebam quod magister iratus erat. (5)

2 magna turba puerorum veniebat. (4)

3 pueri puellas non spectabant. (4)

4 servi ex oppido currebant. (4)

5 cur magister puellas non laudabat? (5)

6 magister puellas non laudabat quod puellae non laborabant. (8)

7 nautae vinum saepe bibebant. (4)

8 puer magistrum non amabat. (4)

9 servi in viis saepe pugnabant. (5)

10 celeriter currebam. (2)

Total: 45

Exercise 16.13

Translate the following into Latin:

1 He used to love.

2 We were seeing.

3 They were ruling.

4 I was.

5 You (pl.) were listening.

6 We were reading.

7 You (sing.) were running.

8 She was praising.

9 They used to walk.

10 I was sending.

1 mark for each question. Total: 10

Exercise 16.14

Translate the following into Latin:

1 The poet was reading.

2 The poets were reading.

3 Flavia was singing.

4 The girls were singing.

5 The slave was fighting.

6 The slaves were fighting.

7 The Romans were attacking.

8 The farmers were working.

9 The horses were drinking.

10 The pupil was watching.

2 marks for each question. Total: 20

Exercise 16.15

Translate the following into Latin:

1 The pupil was reading a book.

2 The pupils were listening to the master.

3 The farmer was carrying a shield.

4 The horse was drinking water.

5 The Greeks were watching the Romans.

3 marks for each question. Total: 15

Exercise 16.16

Translate the following into Latin:

1 The farmers were building a wall.

2 The slave had a daughter.

3 The slave was good.

4 The slaves were good.

5 The master used to frighten the pupils.

3 marks for each question. Total: 15

→ Revision: nouns and verbs

Exercise 16.17

Translate and give the person and number of the following:

1 stas.

2 adest.

3 cupiunt.

4 absunt.

5 bibit.

6 aedificamus.

7 luditis.

8 superant.

9 iubet.

10 constituit.

3 marks for each question. Total: 30

Exercise 16.18

Give and translate the following:

1 The 2nd person plural of the present tense of moveo.

2 The 1st person plural of the present tense of iubeo.

3 The 3rd person plural of the present tense of adsum.

4 The 3rd person singular of the present tense of lego.

5 The 3rd person singular of the present tense of navigo.

6 The 2nd person singular of the imperfect tense of iacio.

7 The 3rd person plural of the imperfect tense of **discedo**.

8 The 1st person singular of the imperfect tense of **oppugno**.

9 The 3rd person singular of the imperfect tense of **absum**.

10 The 1st person plural of the imperfect tense of **ludo**.

2 marks for each question. Total: 20

Exercise 16.19

For this exercise you will need to revise:

- The *he, she, it* endings of the present tenses of **amo** and **moneo** (in other words -at and -et).

- The nominative and accusative singular endings of nouns like **puella** (in other words -a for subject and -am for object).

Instructions
- Put the Latin subject first in the sentence.
- Put the Latin object second in the sentence.
- Put the verb **at the end**.

1 The girl has an arrow.

2 The goddess warns the queen.

3 The queen likes the goddess.

4 The island has a road.

5 The goddess praises the queen.

6 The poet moves the money.

7 The spear frightens the woman.

8 The queen calls the girl.

9 The girl sees the queen.

10 The sailor watches the water.

3 marks for each question. Total: 30

Exercise 16.20

Keeping the same person (1st/2nd/3rd) and number (singular/plural), put the imperfect verbs in this exercise into the present tense, then translate your answer.

1 amabat.

2 monebamus.

3 navigabant.

4 aedificabas.

5 iubebam.

6 stabatis.

7 delebat.

8 flebant.

9 dabamus.

10 respondebat.

2 marks for each question. Total 20

Exercise 16.21

Keeping the same person (1st/2nd/3rd) and number (singular/plural), put the imperfect verbs in this exercise into the present tense, then translate your answer.

1 manebam.

2 ambulabas.

3 habebamus.

4 cantabat.

5 monebant.

6 clamabant.

7 videbat.

8 spectabant.

9 ridebatis.

10 pugnabat.

2 marks for each question. Total: 20

Exercise 17.1

Translate the following passage. Line numbers are given on the left. New words are underlined in the text and their meanings given in the margin.

The wasp

1 Orbilius magister erat. olim in ludo laborabat. multi discipuli aderant. Marcus quoque aderat. discipuli bene laborabant. Orbilius igitur laetus erat.

olim = once (upon a time)
ludus = school

5 subito vespa ludum intravit. Marcus et amici vespam audiverunt, deinde viderunt. non iam laborabant. vespam spectabant. Orbilius, quod discipuli non laborabant, magnopere iratus erat. vespam statim necare igitur constituit.

vespa = wasp
intravit = (he) entered
audiverunt = (they) heard
viderunt = (they) saw

10 vespa iam in magno periculo erat. in muro erat. Orbilius vespam vidit. ad vespam festinavit. vespam necavit. vespam cepit et discipulis ostendit. 'ecce!' Marco et amicis clamavit, 'vespam necavi! nunc laborate, pueri.'

vidit = (he) saw
festinavit = (he) hurried
necavit = (he) killed
cepit = (he) took
ecce! = look!
clamavit = (he) shouted
necavi = I have killed
nunc = now

Total: 75

Exercise 17.2

1 vidit (line 11). Give the Latin subject and Latin object of this verb. (2)

2 ad vespam (line 11). In which case is vespam? Why is this case used? (2)

3 From the passage, give an example of an imperative and quote the line number where it occurs. (1)

Total: 5

→ Perfect tense – 1st conjugation

Exercise 17.3

Translate the following into Latin:

1 I carried.

2 You (pl.) watched.

3 He sailed.

4 We have worked.

5 He fought.

6 You (sing.) sang.

7 He asked.

8 You (pl.) have built.

9 We shouted.

10 She walked.

11 They prepared.

12 We praised.

13 She entered.

14 She sailed.

15 They sang.

16 He worked.

17 We have fought.

18 You (sing.) attacked.

19 They sailed.

20 We entered.

1 mark for each question. Total: 20

Exercise 17.4

Translate the following into Latin:

1 We attacked.

2 I prepared.

3 He loved.

4 You (pl.) hurried.

5 He walked.

6 I entered.

7 She killed.

8 They overcame.

9 We liked.

10 They have attacked.

11 He has hurried.

12 They worked.

13 I have shouted.

14 We have liked.

15 He built.

16 You (pl.) called.

17 They entered.

18 We lived.

19 You (sing.) called.

20 They fought.

1 mark for each question. Total: 20

Exercise 17.5

Translate the following into English:

1 oppidum oppugnavimus.

2 templum intravit.

3 pecuniam portaverunt.

4 servos laudavi.

5 murum aedificavisti.

6 nuntium necavit.

7 puellam amavi.

8 equum necavimus.

9 discipulos laudavit.

10 templum aedificavimus.

2 marks for each question. Total: 20

Exercise 17.6

Translate the following into English:

1 amicos rogaverunt.

2 puellam spectavi.

3 cenam paravisti.

4 templa aedificaverunt.

5 magistrum rogavimus.

6 scuta portaverunt.

7 bella amavit.

8 oppidum oppugnaverunt.

9 puerum laudavistis.

10 dominum necavi.

2 marks for each question. Total: 20

Exercise 17.7

Translate the following into English:

1 amavit.

2 cantavimus.

3 spectavistis.

4 laboravi.

5 vocavistis.

6 navigavi.

7 clamaverunt.

8 ambulavit.

9 vocaverunt.

10 pugnavistis.

11 necavi.

12 paravimus.

13 laudavistis.

14 intravimus.

15 festinavimus.

16 navigavisti.

17 paraverunt.

18 necaverunt.

19 laudavit.

20 festinaverunt.

21 portavit.

22 amavisti.

23 cantavistis.

24 laboraverunt.

25 aedificavi.

26 clamavit.

27 ambulavimus.

28 spectavit.

29 ambulavisti

30 navigaverunt.

1 mark for each question. Total: 30

Exercise 17.8

Translate the following into English:

1 paravistis.

2 vocavimus.

3 laudaverunt.

4 festinavit.

5 aedificaverunt.

6 paravit.

7 spectaverunt.

8 portavimus.

9 vocavisti.

10 navigavit.

11 laboravit.

12 cantavit.

13 amaverunt.

14 portavi.

15 clamavi.

16 pugnavit.

17 aedificavit.

18 oppugnaverunt.

19 spectavi.

20 intravistis.

21 aedificavistis.

22 pugnaverunt.

23 habitavit.

24 vocavit.

25 ambulavi.

26 festinavisti.

27 laudavimus.

28 intraverunt.

29 portavistis.

30 necavit.

1 mark for each question. Total: 30

Exercise 17.9

Translate the following into English:

1 dominus servum laudavit.

2 dominus servos laudavit.

3 Romani oppidum oppugnaverunt.

4 Romani multa oppida aedificaverunt.

5 servus cenam paravit.

6 Romani Graecos superaverunt.

7 nauta murum aedificavit.

8 nuntius proelium spectavit.

9 servi dominum amaverunt.

10 agricola puellam portavit.

11 puella templum spectavit.

12 puer auxilium rogavit.

13 femina cenam bonam paravit.

14 agricola puellam spectavit.

15 Romani muros oppugnaverunt.

16 Romani muros aedificaverunt.

17 Graeci scuta portaverunt.

18 incolae Romanos superaverunt.

19 vir villam intravit.

20 sagitta virum necavit.

3 marks for each question. Total: 60

➜ Perfect tense – 2nd conjugation

Exercise 17.10

Translate the following into Latin:

1 We warned.

2 You (sing.) frightened.

3 He has had. *to have, I have- habeo*

4 They held.

5 I frightened.

6 I have been afraid.

7 She held.

8 He held.

9 They had.

10 You (pl.) have frightened.

11 We feared.

12 We have feared.

13 We have had.

14 You (sing.) have had.

15 She warned.

16 They feared.

17 We had.

18 You (sing.) have warned.

19 I have held.

20 He has been afraid.

1 mark for each question. Total: 20

Exercise 17.11

For this exercise you will need to revise:

● The *he, she, it* endings of the present tenses of **amo** and **moneo** (in other words -at and -et)

● The nominative and accusative singular endings of nouns like **dominus**, **puer**, **magister** and **bellum**.

Instructions
● Put the Latin subject first in the sentence.
● Put the Latin object second in the sentence.
● Put the verb **at the end**.

1 The slave has a friend.

2 The friend likes the slave.

3 The wind frightens the boy.

4 The boy fears the wind.

5 The master orders the messenger.

6 The messenger kills the master.

7 The god likes gold.

8 The boy fears danger.

9 Danger frightens the boy.

10 The horse likes food.

3 marks for each question. Total: 30

Exercise 17.12

Keeping the same person and number, put the following verbs – which are all in the perfect tense – into the present tense, then translate your answer.

→ 1 amavi. — amo   I love

2 monuit.

3 paravimus.

4 habuisti.

5 tenuimus.

6 navigavit.

7 terruerunt.

8 portaverunt.

9 spectavistis.

10 timuisti.

2 marks for each question. Total: 20

Exercise 18.1

Translate the following passage. Line numbers are given on the left. New words are underlined in the text and their meanings given in the margin.

Caught in the act

1 olim Flavia cenam in villa parare cupiebat.
    Marcus cenas Flaviae amabat. in villa <u>autem</u>
    Flavia multum cibum non habebat. in oppidum
    igitur <u>ire</u> et cibum ibi <u>emere</u> constituit. itaque
5 e villa <u>exiit</u> et per viam ad oppidum ambulavit.

    in via <u>taberna</u> erat. Flavia, ubi ad <u>tabernam</u>
    venit, intrare et vinum <u>emere</u> constituit. ubi
    autem <u>tabernam</u> intravit, <u>rem horribilem</u>
    <u>vidit</u>. Marcum <u>vidit</u>. <u>ille</u> puellam <u>basiabat</u>!
10 Marcus, ubi Flaviam <u>vidit</u>, statim <u>rubuit</u>.
    'Marce!' <u>clamavit</u> Flavia. 'quid facis?' 'nihil
    facio,' <u>respondit</u> Marcus. '<u>haec</u> Valeria est.
    Valeria <u>amica</u> mea nova est.' 'puer <u>horribilis</u>
    es, Marce,' inquit Flavia. 'te <u>odi</u>.' e <u>taberna</u> <u>flens</u>
15 <u>cucurrit</u> et ad villam festinavit. irata erat.
    magnopere irata erat.

autem = however
ire = to go
emere = to buy
exiit = (she) went out
taberna = pub
rem horribilem = a
dreadful sight
vidit = (she/he) saw
ille = he
basio (1) = I kiss
rubuit = he blushed
clamavit = (she) shouted
respondit = (he) replied
haec = this
amica = girlfriend
horribilis = dreadful
odi = I hate
flens = crying
cucurrit = she ran

Total: 100

Exercise 18.2

1 From the passage, give an example of (and quote the line number):

   (i)   A verb in the imperfect tense.   (1)

   (ii) A verb in the perfect tense.   (1)

   (iii) A verb in the present tense.   (1)

   (iv) An infinitive.   (1)

2 erat (line 6). Give the person and number of this verb. Give the
   1st person singular of its present tense. Translate erat.   (4)

3 puer (line 13). Explain the connection between this word and the
   English word *puerile*.   (2)

4 taberna (line 14). In which case is this noun? Why is this case used?   (2)

Total: 12

→ Perfect tense – 3rd conjugation

Exercise 18.3

Translate the following into Latin:

1 We ruled.

2 You (sing.) said.

3 He has led. (I lead duco)

4 I have said.

5 They said.

6 They ruled.

7 You (pl.) led.

8 He said.

9 I led.

10 We said.

1 mark for each question. Total: 10

→ Perfect tense – 4th conjugation

Exercise 18.4

Translate the following into Latin:

1 They heard.

2 You (sing.) slept

3 I heard.

4 They have punished.

5 He slept.

6 They have slept.

7 She has slept.

8 He punished.

9 We punished.

10 You (pl.) heard.

1 mark for each question. Total: 10

→ Revision: adjectives, nouns and verbs

Exercise 18.5

Put these into the plural and translate your answer:

1 servus fessus.

2 puella bona.

3 femina perterrita.

4 templum novum.

5 agricola iratus.

2 + 2 marks for each question. Total: 20

Exercise 18.6

Put these into the singular and translate your answer:

1 puellae pulchrae.

2 servi validi.

3 bella mala.

4 pueri mali.

5 nautae boni.

2 + 2 marks for each question. Total: 20

Exercise 18.7

Put these verbs into the plural and translate your answer:

1 habet.

2 ambulabas.

3 amavisti.

4 rexit.

5 festinabam.

2 + 2 marks for each question. Total: 20

Exercise 18.8

Put these verbs into the singular and translate your answer:

1 currunt.

2 timebant.

3 audiverunt.

4 audiunt.

5 monuerunt.

1 + 1 marks for each question. Total: 10

Exercise 18.9

Put these sentences into the plural and translate your answer:

1 discipulus magistrum audivit.

2 nauta oppidum oppugnavit.

3 puella puerum amavit.

4 dominus servum punivit.

5 puer ad villam ambulabat.

3 + 3 marks for each question. Total: 30

Exercise 18.10

Put these sentences into the singular and translate your answer:

1 servi dormiverunt.   (2+2)

2 servi libros portaverunt.   (3+3)

3 ancillae cenas parabant.   (3+3)

4 discipuli in oppida currunt.   (3+3)

5 magistri verba mala dixerunt.   (4+4)

Total: 30

Exercise 18.11

For this exercise you will need to revise:

● The *he, she, it* endings of the present tenses of **amo** and **moneo** (in other words -at and -et)

● The nominative and accusative singular endings of nouns like **dominus, puer, magister** and **bellum**.

Instructions

- Put the Latin subject first in the sentence.
- Put the Latin object second in the sentence.
- Put the verb **at the end.**

Translate the following into Latin:

1 The messenger has a horse.

2 The slave builds a wall.

3 The god likes the temple.

4 The wind destroys the town.

5 The field gives food.

6 The slave has a field.

7 The master praises the slave.

8 The slave likes wine.

9 The boy fears the battle.

10 The horse likes the master.

3 marks for each question. Total: 30

(Now try Test 4 at the back of the book.)

→ Revision: perfect tense

Exercises 19.1 and 19.2 are revision exercises on the perfect tense. The following verbs are used in the exercises. The perfect tenses are in **bold** print, because these are the forms you will need in these exercises.

advise	moneo, monere, **monui** (2)
be afraid	timeo, timere, **timui** (2)
carry	porto, portare, **portavi** (1)
fear	timeo, timere, **timui** (2)
frighten	terreo, terrere, **terrui** (2)
have	habeo, habere, **habui** (2)
hear	audio, audire, **audivi** (4)
hurry	festino, festinare, **festinavi** (1)
lead	duco, ducere, **duxi** (3)
listen to	audio, audire, **audivi** (4)
look (at)	specto, spectare, **spectavi** (1)
punish	punio, punire, **punivi** (4)
rule	rego, regere, **rexi** (3)
say	dico, dicere, **dixi** (3)
shout	clamo, clamare, **clamavi** (1)
sleep	dormio, dormire, **dormivi** (4)
warn	moneo, monere, **monui** (2)
watch	specto, spectare, **spectavi** (1)

Exercise 19.1

Translate the following into Latin:

1 You (pl.) ruled.

2 I led.

3 We slept.

4 We shouted.

5 You (sing.) frightened.

6 He frightened

7 They ruled.

8 She shouted.

9 You (sing.) slept.

10 You (pl.) shouted.

11 I slept.

12 I shouted.

13 You (pl.) frightened.

14 He carried.

15 You (sing.) ruled.

16 You (sing.) had.

17 We heard.

18 You (pl.) slept.

19 I warned.

20 You (pl.) hurried.

1 mark for each question. Total: 20

Exercise 19.2

Translate the following into Latin:

1 They carried.

2 You (pl.) carried.

3 They frightened.

4 I ruled.

5 We led.

6 You (sing.) carried.

7 They watched.

8 I frightened.

9 He hurried.

10 I watched.

11 I heard.

12 They warned.

13 We punished.

14 They hurried.

15 You (pl.) feared.

16 You (sing.) feared.

17 We said.

18 They shouted.

19 You (sing.) hurried.

20 You (sing.) heard.

1 mark for each question. Total: 20

Exercise 19.3

Translate the following into English:

1 habuimus.

2 tenuerunt.

3 pugnavi.

4 dixit.

5 duxit.

6 dormivisti.

7 duximus.

8 rexerunt.

9 terruerunt.

10 timuisti.

11 laboravi.

12 monuistis.

13 habui.

14 duxisti.

15 dormivit.

16 reximus.

17 punivisti.

18 diximus.

19 fui.

20 festinavimus.

1 mark for each question. Total: 20

Chapter 19

Exercise 19.4

Translate the following into English:

1 discipuli dormiverunt.

2 verba audivimus.

3 servum punivisti.

4 terram rexi.

5 deam timuimus.

6 magistri boni fuerunt.

7 oppidum oppugnavimus.

8 discipulum laudavi.

9 gladios tenuistis.

10 discipuli timuerunt.

2 marks for each question. Total: 20

Exercise 19.5

Translate the following into English:

1 nautae oppidum oppugnaverunt.

2 discipulus dominum timuit.

3 servus equum duxit.

4 multa verba dixit.

5 dominus servos punivit.

6 pueri servum laudaverunt.

7 discipuli nuntium audiverunt.

8 magister discipulos terruit.

9 puer gladium tenuit.

10 servi equos duxerunt.

3 marks for each question. Total: 30

→ Irregular perfect tenses

You have already met these verbs in the perfect tense.

conjugation	present		perfect	
1	amo	I love	amavi	I loved
2	moneo	I warn	monui	I warned
3	rego	I rule	rexi	I ruled
4	audio	I hear	audivi	I heard
irregular	sum	I am	fui	I was

Here are some more common verbs with their perfects. Note that these perfect forms simply have to be learnt by heart.

conjugation	present		perfect	
1	do	I give	dedi	I gave
1	sto	I stand	steti	I stood
2	deleo	I destroy	delevi	I destroyed
2	iubeo	I order	iussi	I ordered
2	maneo	I stay	mansi	I stayed
2	moveo	I move	movi	I moved
2	respondeo	I answer	respondi	I answered
2	rideo	I laugh	risi	I laughed
2	video	I see	vidi	I saw
3	bibo	I drink	bibi	I drank
3	constituo	I decide	constitui	I decided
3	consumo	I eat	consumpsi	I ate
3	curro	I run	cucurri	I ran
3	dico	I say	dixi	I said
3	discedo	I depart	discessi	I departed
3	duco	I lead	duxi	I led
3	lego	I read	legi	I read
3	ludo	I play	lusi	I played
3	mitto	I send	misi	I sent
3	ostendo	I show	ostendi	I showed
3	pono	I put	posui	I put
3	scribo	I write	scripsi	I wrote
$3\frac{1}{2}$	capio	I take	cepi	I took
$3\frac{1}{2}$	cupio	I want	cupivi	I wanted
$3\frac{1}{2}$	facio	I do, I make	feci	I did, I made
$3\frac{1}{2}$	fugio	I flee	fugi	I fled
$3\frac{1}{2}$	iacio	I throw	ieci	I threw
4	dormio	I sleep	dormivi	I slept
4	venio	I come	veni	I came

Exercise 19.6

Using the verbs in the table above, translate the following into Latin:

1 He gave.

2 They led.

3 I slept.

4 You (sing.) made.

5 They fled.

6 She said.

7 They ran.

8 You (pl.) stood.

9 He stayed.

10 He led.

11 We slept.

12 You (pl.) made.

13 They made.

14 We led.

15 I said.

16 You (sing.) stayed.

17 I gave.

18 He made.

19 They saw.

20 You (pl.) said.

21 I made.

22 She heard.

23 They stood.

24 They were.

25 He stood.

26 We ran.

27 You (sing.) fled.

28 You (pl.) stayed.

29 We made.

30 You (sing.) saw.

1 mark for each question. Total: 30

Exercise 19.7

Using the verbs in the table on the previous page, translate the following into Latin:

1 I ran.

2 We saw.

3 He destroyed.

4 They destroyed.

5 They said.

6 They gave.

7 You (sing.) stood.

8 We stayed.

9 He slept.

10 She fled.

11 I saw.

12 You (sing.) led.

13 They stayed.

14 We fled.

15 I destroyed.

16 He saw.

17 You (pl.) destroyed.

18 He ran.

19 We gave.

20 They slept.

21 They moved.

22 We came.

23 He ordered.

24 They wrote.

25 You (sing.) sent.

26 They answered.

27 They threw.

28 You (pl.) laughed.

29 He put.

30 I showed.

1 mark for each question. Total: 30

Exercise 19.8

Using the verbs in the table on the previous page, translate the following into Latin.

1 He came.

2 She wanted.

3 He ate.

4 They departed.

5 He took.

6 He decided.

7 They played.

8 They drank.

9 They put.

10 You (sing.) drank.

11 We played.

12 You (pl.) warned.

13 We wanted.

14 He departed.

15 I played.

16 You (pl.) ate.

17 I took.

18 He wrote.

19 They decided.

20 They came.

21 He drank.

22 We ate.

23 She read.

24 I came.

25 They wanted.

26 She sent.

27 You (pl.) took.

28 I threw.

29 We decided.

30 We wrote.

1 mark for each question. Total: 30

Exercise 19.9

Translate the following into Latin:

1 The slave has a sword.

2 The slave is holding the sword.

3 The master sees danger.

4 The messenger is carrying wine.

5 The sword kills the boy.

6 The wind destroys the wall.

7 The master warns the boy.

8 The boy fears the master.

9 The slave looks at the temple.

10 The god looks at the sky.

3 marks for each question. Total: 30

Exercise 19.10

Keeping the same person and number, put the following verbs into the present tense, then translate your answer:

1 iussi.

2 stetit.

3 flebat.

4 mansit.

5 navigabat.

6 dedimus.

7 stabamus.

8 respondit.

9 clamavistis.

10 deleverunt.

1 + 1 mark for each question. Total: 20

Exercise 20.1

Translate the following passage. Line numbers are given on the left. New words are underlined in the text and their meanings given in the margin.

Marcus gets his comeuppance

1   Flavia e <u>taberna</u> cucurrit. flebat sed
    magnopere irata erat. Marcus et Valeria in
    <u>taberna</u> manserunt. Marcus Valeriam
    spectavit. Valeria Marcum spectavit. diu nihil
5   dixerunt. tandem Valeria Marcum rogavit:
    'quis erat <u>illa</u> puella, Marce?' Marcus
    respondit: '<u>illa</u> puella Flavia erat. <u>amica</u> mea
    est ... erat.'

    'amica tua?!' clamavit Valeria. irata erat.
10 '<u>duas</u>ne <u>amicas</u> habes, Marce? <u>et</u> Flaviam <u>et</u> me?
    responde, Marce! statim responde! irata sum.'

    Marcus tamen Valeriae respondere non
    cupivit. iterum <u>rubuit</u>.

    'te non amo, Marce,' inquit Valeria. 'puer
15 malus es. tu amicus meus non es. <u>vale</u>!' ubi
    <u>haec</u> verba dixit, Marcum <u>pulsavit</u> et irata e
    <u>taberna</u> festinavit.

    Marcus in <u>taberna</u> <u>attonitus</u> manebat. <u>solus</u>
    erat.

Margin notes:
taberna = pub

illa = that

amica = girlfriend
duas = two
et ... et ... = both ... and ...

rubuit = he blushed

vale! = goodbye!
haec = these
pulso, -are (1) = I thump
attonitus = amazed

solus = alone

Total: 100

Exercise 20.2

1   From the passage, give an example (and quote the line number)
    of the following:

    (i)   A verb in the perfect tense.   (1)

    (ii)   A verb in the imperfect tense.   (1)

    (iii) An imperative.   (1)

    (iv)   An infinitive.   (1)

2   manserunt (line 3). Give the person, number and the 1st person singular
    of the present tense of this verb.   (3)

3   amicus (line 15). Is the gender of this noun masculine, feminine or neuter? (1)

4   taberna (line 18). In which case is this noun? Why is this case used? (2)

Total: 10

→ Revision

Exercise 20.3

Translate the following into English:

1 dedi.
2 discessit.
3 misisti.
4 delevistis.
5 risisti.
6 iussimus.
7 cucurristi.
8 fecistis.
9 manserunt.
10 fuit.
11 cepit.
12 audivit.
13 feci.
14 rexit.
15 iecit.
16 respondit.
17 fuimus.
18 dedisti.
19 fecerunt.
20 mansimus.
21 stetimus.
22 fecimus.
23 vidisti.
24 dederunt.
25 biberunt.
26 veni.
27 delevimus.
28 luserunt.
29 bibisti.
30 dixerunt.

1 mark for each question. Total: 30

Exercise 20.4

Translate the following into English:

1 miserunt.
2 riserunt.
3 discesserunt
4 iussit.
5 dixit.
6 scripserunt.
7 vidi.
8 ceperunt.
9 deleverunt.
10 fecisti.
11 dedit.
12 iussi.
13 cucurri.
14 stetit.
15 iussisti.
16 fecit.
17 dixi.
18 misit.
19 risit.
20 discessimus.
21 cucurrit.
22 iusserunt.
23 posuit.
24 vidit.
25 steterunt.
26 respondi.

Chapter 20

27 cucurrerunt.

28 dedimus.

29 mansit.

30 vidimus.

1 mark for each question. Total: 30

Exercise 20.5

Translate the following into English:

1 vir stetit.

2 equus cucurrit.

3 puellae manserunt.

4 auxilium venit.

5 servi dormiverunt.

6 magister respondit.

7 Romani fugerunt.

8 nautae discesserunt.

9 regina risit.

10 dominus constituit.

2 marks for each question. Total: 20

Exercise 20.6

Translate the following into English:

1 libros legi.

2 equum duxisti.

3 librum scripsi.

4 scutum cepit.

5 hastam ieci.

6 reginam vidit.

7 vinum bibimus.

8 murum moverunt.

9 cibum consumpsistis.

10 templa deleverunt.

2 marks for each question. Total: 20

Exercise 20.7

Translate the following into Latin:

1 The man drank.

2 The girl slept.

3 The Romans came.

4 The sailor read.

5 The pupils laughed.

6 The slave fled.

7 The allies departed.

8 The boy answered.

9 The friends stayed.

10 The messenger ran.

2 marks for each question. Total: 20

Exercise 20.8

Translate the following into Latin:

1 I have held a shield.

2 They loved the girl.

3 We read the book.

4 He attacked the town.

5 You (sing.) saw the place.

6 They destroyed the villas.

7 They drank the water.

8 We sent the food.

9 I took the money.

10 I have been angry.

2 marks for each question. Total: 20

Exercise 20.9

Translate the following into Latin:

1 The master has written a book.

2 The slaves moved the food.

3 The Greeks destroyed the villa.

4 The pupil threw water.

5 The sailors took the town.

3 marks for each question. Total: 15

Exercise 20.10

Translate the following into Latin:

1 The friends ran out of the temple. (4)

2 The woman read a book to the boys. (4)

3 The sailor decided to drink wine. (4)

4 The Romans destroyed the wall in the battle. (5)

5 The farmers led the horse out of the field. (5)

Total: 22

Exercise 20.11

Translate the following into English:

1 nauta ab insula navigavit. (4)

2 puellae bene dormiverunt. (3)

3 magister librum bonum scripsit. (4)

4 reginam audivimus. (2)

5 servi ex oppido fugerunt. (4)

6 puer parvus in viam cucurrit. (5)

7 puer in muro stetit. (3)

8 quid fecistis, pueri? (3)

9 vir hastam iecit. (3)

10 ad oppidum celeriter venimus. (4)

Total: 35

Exercise 20.12

Translate the following into English:

1 librum non legistis, discipuli. (4)

2 ancillae aquam et vinum biberunt. (5)

3 multi servi in villa laboraverunt. (5)

4 dominus multam pecuniam servo dedit. (5)

5 magister discipulos laborare iussit. (4)

6 Romani murum oppugnare constituerunt. (4)

7 vir gladium cepit et in proelium cucurrit. (7)

8 Graeci multas hastas in Romanos iecerunt. (6)

9 discipuli verba magistri non audiverunt. (5)

10 servus equos ex agris duxit. (5)

Total: 50

Exercise 20.13

Translate the following into English:

1 librum bonum ad amicum misi. (5)

2 dominus multa verba servis dixit. (5)

3 Valeria Marcum rogavit: 'cur non respondisti?' (6)

4 bonus esse constitui. (3)

5 pueri cum amicis in via luserunt. (6)

6 periculum nautas terruit. (3)

7 aurum magistro ostendimus. (3)

8 servus pecuniam capere cupivit. (4)

9 pecuniam in templo deorum posuimus. (5)

10 Graeci e periculo non fugerunt. (5)

Total: 45

Exercise 20.14

For this exercise you will need to revise:

- The *he, she, it* endings of the present tenses of **amo** and **moneo** (in other words -at and -et).

- The nominative and accusative singular endings of nouns like **dominus, puer, magister** and **bellum**.

> **Instructions**
> - Put the Latin subject first in the sentence.
> - Put the Latin object second in the sentence.
> - Put the verb **at the end**.

1 The farmer has a horse.

2 The woman has a slave.

3 The girl likes the master.

4 The master likes the girl.

5 The danger frightens the maidservant.

6 The maidservant fears danger.

7 The sailor looks at the sword.

8 The queen is holding the sword.

9 The sword kills the daughter.

10 The poet likes wine.

3 marks for each question. Total: 30

Present, imperfect and perfect tenses

Exercise 21.1

Translate the following into English:

1	currimus.	16	misisti
2	currebamus.	17	mittis.
3	cucurrimus.	18	mittebas.
4	pugnavi.	19	delebam.
5	pugnabam.	20	delevi.
6	pugno.	21	deleo.
7	videbant.	22	scribit.
8	vident.	23	scripsit.
9	viderunt.	24	scribebat.
10	auditis.	25	dabamus.
11	audivistis.	26	damus.
12	audiebatis.	27	dedimus.
13	est.	28	rident.
14	erat.	29	riserunt.
15	fuit.	30	ridebant.

1 mark for each question. Total: 30

Exercise 21.2

Translate the following into English:

1	legunt.	8	movebas.
2	iecimus.	9	cupiebamus.
3	oppugnabant.	10	consumpsimus.
4	aedificaverunt.	11	stetit.
5	iussit.	12	bibi.
6	superant.	13	sedebant.
7	constituerunt.	14	respondet.

15 respondit.

16 rogavi.

17 timeo.

18 terrebamus.

19 vident.

20 intrabat.

21 pugnaverunt.

22 laborabat.

23 clamamus.

24 discesserunt.

25 punis.

26 scripsi.

27 fleo.

28 dedit.

29 faciebant.

30 erant.

1 mark for each question. Total: 30

Exercise 21.3

Translate the following into Latin:

1 We sing.

2 We sang.

3 We were singing.

4 I see.

5 I saw.

6 I was seeing.

7 They ran.

8 They were running.

9 They are running.

10 You (pl.) come.

11 You (pl.) came.

12 You (pl.) were coming.

13 They are.

14 They have been.

15 They were.

16 We were sleeping.

17 We slept.

18 We sleep.

19 He takes.

20 He took.

21 He was taking.

22 You (sing.) were leading.

23 You (sing.) led.

24 You (sing.) lead.

25 They destroyed.

26 They destroy.

27 They were destroying.

28 I was standing.

29 I stand.

30 I stood.

1 mark for each question. Total: 30

Exercise 21.4

Translate the following into Latin:

1 He was.

2 We see.

3 We saw.

4 You (sing.) write.

5 You (sing.) wrote.

6 He comes.

7 He was coming.

8 I am.

9 He was leading.

10 They send.

11 I was giving.

12 They came.

13 She called.

14 We were killing.

15 We were laughing.

16 They laughed.

17 I was deciding.

18 I decided.

19 We attack.

20 They were throwing

21 You (pl.) were sailing.

22 He is warning.

23 They were eating.

24 We departed.

25 They lead.

26 They sent.

27 We were ruling.

28 I ask.

29 You (pl.) hurried.

30 They were praising.

1 mark for each question. Total: 30

Exercise 21.5

Write the answer and translate the following:

1 The 3rd person singular of the present tense of amo.

2 The 2nd person plural of the perfect tense of scribo.

3 The 1st person plural of the imperfect tense of laudo.

4 The 3rd person plural of the perfect tense of iacio.

5 The 2nd person singular of the imperfect tense of oppugno.

6 The 1st person singular of the present tense of navigo.

7 The 3rd person singular of the imperfect tense of constituo.

8 The 3rd person plural of the perfect tense of moveo.

9 The 2nd person plural of the present tense of cupio.

10 The 1st person plural of the imperfect tense of sto.

2 marks for each question. Total: 20

Exercise 21.6

Write the anwer and translate the following:

1 The 1st person singular of the present tense of bibo.

2 The 3rd person singular of the imperfect tense of adsum.

3 The 3rd person plural of the perfect tense of lego.

4 The 2nd person singular of the perfect tense of discedo.

5 The 2nd person plural of the imperfect tense of deleo.

6 The 1st person plural of the imperfect tense of punio.

7 The 1st person singular of the present tense of fleo.

8 The 2nd person singular of the perfect tense of **scribo**.

9 The 3rd person plural of the perfect tense of **dormio**.

10 The 1st person plural of the imperfect tense of **mitto**.

2 marks for each question. Total: 20

Exercise 21.7

Write the answer and translate the following:

1 The 3rd person singular of the present tense of **canto**.

2 The 1st person singular of the imperfect tense of **duco**.

3 The 1st person plural of the perfect tense of **venio**.

4 The 2nd person plural of the perfect tense of **audio**.

5 The 2nd person plural of the imperfect tense of **intro**.

6 The 3rd person singular of the present tense of **respondeo**.

7 The 2nd person plural of the imperfect tense of **rogo**.

8 The 1st person plural of the imperfect tense of **timeo**.

9 The 2nd person singular of the perfect tense of **habeo**.

10 The 3rd person singular of the perfect tense of **pono**.

2 marks for each question. Total: 20

Exercise 21.8

Translate the following and then give the 1st person singular present:

1 iecerunt.

2 oppugnabant.

3 navigatis.

4 aedificamus.

5 iussit.

6 superabant.

7 movebam.

8 constituit.

9 cupivimus.

10 stant.

2 marks for each question. Total: 20

Exercise 21.9

Translate the following and then give the 1st person singular present:

1 biberunt.

2 consumit.

3 lego.

4 discessisti.

5 iussistis.

6 aberat.

7 adest.

8 deleverunt.

9 puniunt.

10 scribebam.

2 marks for each question. Total: 20

Exercise 21.10

Translate the following and then give the 1st person singular present:

1 das.

2 ostendis.

3 dormiebamus.

4 veni.

5 audimus.

6 cucurristis.

7 rexit.

8 mittebamus.

9 dixit.

10 sedebas.

2 marks for each question. Total: 20

Exercise 21.11

Translate the following into Latin:

1 The slave is carrying water.

2 The man destroys the wall.

3 The messenger praises the queen.

4 The queen calls the slave.

5 The slave likes the queen.

6 The queen orders the messenger.

7 The messenger has a daughter.

8 The crowd is building a temple.

9 The god gives money.

10 The goddess likes the god.

3 marks for each question. Total: 30

Exercise 21.12

Translate the following into Latin:

1 The boy fears the battle.

2 The battle frightens the boy.

3 The sailor warns the queen.

4 The messenger enters the town.

5 The crowd is looking at the sky.

6 The spear frightens the man.

7 The wave destroys the wall.

8 The crowd attacks the temple.

9 The son has a sword.

10 The poet sees the book.

3 marks for each question. Total: 30

Exercise 21.13

Keeping the same person and number, put the following verbs into the present tense, then translate your answer:

1 festinaverunt.

2 monebatis.

3 timebat.

4 dederunt.

5 amabamus.

6 clamavit.

7 delebamus.

8 terruimus.

9 portabas.

10 vidimus.

2 marks for each question. Total: 20

(Now try Test 5 at the back of the book.)

Test exercises

Test 1 (Chapter 7)

Read and study the following passage, then answer the questions which follow it.

Aurelia and Valeria enjoy dinner

1   Aurelia puella Romana est. in villa habitat. Aurelia
    amicam habet. amica est Valeria. Valeria quoque
    puella Romana est.

    Aurelia Valeriam amat. Valeriam ad cenam invitat.
5   cena bona est. puellae laetae sunt. rident.

in = in
amica = girlfriend

ad = to
invito (1) = I invite
bona = good
laetae = happy

1   In line 1 what are we told about Aurelia?   (2)

2   In line 1 where does Aurelia live?   (1)

3   Translate into good English lines 4-5 (Aurelia ... rident).   (10)

4   amat (line 4). Give the Latin subject and the Latin object of this verb.   (2)

Total: 15

Test 2 (Chapter 11)

Read and study the following passage, then answer the questions which follow it.

Valerius and Gaius

1   Valerius est vir Romanus. multam pecuniam et
    multos servos habet. servi in agris semper laborant.
    dominum timent.

    Gaius est servus. est servus ignavus. in agris Valerii
5   numquam laborat. Gaius Valerium non amat. Valerius
    Gaium non amat. Valerius Gaium saepe punit quod in
    agris numquam laborat.

multam = much, a lot of
multos = many

ignavus = lazy

1   In lines 1–2 what things are we told Valerius has?   (2)

2   In line 2 where do Valerius' slaves work?   (1)

3   In line 3 what are the feelings of the slaves towards their master?   (1)

4   Translate into good English lines 4–7 (Gaius ... laborat).   (15)

5   est (line 4). Give the 1st person singular of this verb.   (1)

6   Valerii (line 4). In which case is this noun?   (1)

7   amat (line 6). Give the person and number of this verb.   (2)

8   agris (line 7). In which case is this noun? Why is this case used?   (2)

Total: 25

Test 3 (Chapter 14)

Read and study the following passage, then answer the questions which follow it.

Orbilius deals with Publius

1 Orbilius magister est. in <u>ludo</u> laborat. multi discipuli
in <u>ludo</u> Orbilii sunt. discipuli boni sunt. semper   ludo = school
laborant. Orbilius, quod discipuli bene laborant,
laetus est.
5 unus e discipulis tamen, Publius, numquam laborat.
numquam verba Orbilii audit. in <u>ludo</u> semper ludit.
Orbilius, ubi Publium videt, iratus est. 'statim labora,
puer!' clamat.

Publius, ubi verba Orbilii audit, magnopere
10 perterritus est. iam laborat.

1	In line 1 what is Orbilius' occupation?	(1)
2	In lines 1–2 how many people are there in the school?	(1)
3	In lines 2–3 what are we told about the pupils?	(2)
4	In line 4 what is Orbilius' reaction to this?	(1)
5	Translate into good English lines 5–8 (unus … clamat).	(15)
6	verba (line 9). Give the gender of this noun.	(1)
7	audit (line 9). Give the Latin object of this verb.	(1)
8	From lines 9–10 give an example of an adjective.	(1)
9	est (line 10). Give the person and number of this verb.	(2)

Total: 25

Test 4 (Chapter 18)

Read and study the following passage, then answer the questions which follow it.

Julius Caesar and Britain

1 Iulius Caesar Romanus notus et clarus erat.
olim <u>Britanniam</u> capere constituit. multas   Britannia, -ae f. = Britain
<u>copias</u> igitur celeriter paravit et trans mare   copiae f.pl. = troops, forces
ad <u>Britanniam</u> navigavit.
5 Romani, ubi ad <u>Britanniam</u> venerunt, contra incolas
pugnaverunt. incolae bene pugnaverunt. Romani
quoque bene pugnaverunt. incolas <u>Britanniae</u>
tamen statim superare non <u>poterant</u>.   poterant = (they) were able

Iulius Caesar igitur laetus non erat. e <u>Britannia</u>
10 discedere constituit.

1	In line 1 which two things are we told about Julius Caesar?	(2)
2	In line 2 what did he decide to do?	(2)
3	In lines 3–4 after preparing his forces, what did he do?	(2)
4	Translate into good English lines 5–8 (Romani … poterant).	(15)
5	From lines 9–10 give an example of an adjective and an infinitive.	(2)

6   erat (line 9). Give the tense of this verb. Give the 1st person singular of the
    present tense of this verb.   (2)

7   Britannia (line 9). In which case is this noun? Why is this case used?   (2)

8   constituit (line 10). Give the person, number and tense of this verb.   (3)

Total: 30

Test 5 (Chapter 21)

Read and study the following passage, then answer the questions which follow it.

The wooden horse of Troy

1   Graeci contra Troianos diu pugnabant. irati erant   Troiani = Trojans
    quod oppidum Troiam capere non poterant.   poterant = they were able
    Ulixes igitur, Graecus clarus, amicos equum magnum   Ulixes = Ulysses (a Greek)
    aedificare iussit. Graeci, ubi equum fecerunt, eum   eum = it
5   prope oppidum Troiam posuerunt. deinde
    discesserunt. Troiani equum in oppidum duxerunt.
    milites Graeci tamen in equo erant. dum Troiani   milites = soldiers
    dormiunt, Graeci de equo descenderunt et multos   dum = while
    Troianos necaverunt. sic Graeci Troiam ceperunt.   descendo, -ere, descendi
                                                          (3) = I climb down

1   In line 1 for how long did the fighting go on?   (1)

2   In line 1 what were the feelings of the Greeks?   (1)

3   In line 2 why did they feel this way?   (2)

4   Translate into good English lines 3–6 (Ulixes … duxerunt).   (20)

5   From the passage give an example of an infinitive.   (1)

6   equo (line 8). In which case is this noun? Why is this case used?   (2)

7   descenderunt (line 8). In which tense is this verb?   (1)

8   ceperunt (line 9). Give the person of this verb. Give the 1st person
    singular of the present tense of this verb.   (2)

Total: 30

Grammar check

Make sure that you know the meanings of the following grammatical terms.

adjective	a word which describes a noun, e.g. bonus *(good)* or iratus *(angry)*
adverb	a word which describes a verb, e.g. saepe *(often)* celeriter *(quickly)*
cardinal number	a number like unus *(one)*, duo *(two)*, tres *(three)* [beware of confusing this with **ordinal number**]
case	nominative (subject), vocative (person spoken to), accusative (object), genitive *(of)*, dative *(to or for)* or ablative *(by, with, from)*
conjugation	a family of verbs which behave in the same way
conjunction	a joining word, like et *(and)* or sed *(but)*
declension	a family of nouns or adjectives which behave in the same way
gender	whether a noun is masculine, feminine or neuter
imperative	a command – ordering someone to do something – e.g. ama! *(love! – singular imperative)*; **amate!** *(love! – plural imperative)*
imperfect tense	a continuous action in the past
infinitive	a *to*-word; in Latin they usually end in -re, e.g. amare, *to love*, [but beware of the irregular esse, *to be*]
noun	the name of a person, place or thing
number	singular or plural
object	the person being done to – the receiver of the action
ordinal number	a number like primus *(first)*, secundus *(second)*, tertius *(third)* [beware of confusing this with **cardinal number** – think of putting things in order]
perfect tense	a single, completed action in the past
person	1st, 2nd or 3rd – the person or persons doing the action:

1st person singular = *I*	1st person plural = *we*
2nd person singular = *you*	2nd person plural = *you*
3rd person singular = *he, she, it*	3rd person plural = *they*

preposition	a little word which precedes a noun, like in *(in)*, cum *(with)*
present tense	an action taking place **now**, in the present
subject	the doer of the action
verb	a doing word